MOUNTAINMEN

Our Alberta Heritage Series II

By Jacques Hamilton

Illustrated by Dianne Bersea

COMMISSIONED BY CALGARY POWER LTD.
CALGARY, ALBERTA, CANADA

Printed in Canada

INTRODUCTION

The people examined in this volume, MOUNTAINMEN, show a determined bid to carve their living from the mountains. The beauty and excitement of the Rockies is told in spirited tales of both tragedies and dreams that lead man to challenge the valleys and peaks of our western border. You will see in these stories the determination and dedication that we also see today in those that make Alberta their home.

We at Calgary Power trust that you will find the same enjoyment in reading these stories as we have experienced in finding and recording them.

—A. W. Howard,
Chairman of the Board
Calgary Power Ltd.

It is impossible to name them all here, but we would like to express our gratitude to the hundreds of Albertans who so graciously gave their time, their help and their rare records to make this project possible.

—*J. H.*

CONTENTS

FOREWORD

"At last the Rocky Mountains came in sight like shining white clouds in the horizon."

— DAVID THOMPSON

* * *

Wong-Tai is an old man now. More than a hundred years old—though just how much older not even he can remember anymore.

Every day, when the weather lets him, he takes a short walk through the streets of downtown Calgary.

Few who see him know him. Fewer still recognize him as a frail, human link with a part of Alberta history that is far older than Alberta itself.

Wong-Tai is the last survivor of the Chinese laborers who struggled, and often died, to build the mountain section of the Canadian Pacific Railway.

All he remembers of those days is that the pay was 75 cents a day. And that when the job was finished he was given a gift of his pick and shovel.

Wong-Tai may seem a strange place to begin a selection of stories about Alberta's "Mountainmen." Much came before what he did and much came after.

But the rails that Wong-Tai helped lay became the fragile thread that finally bound Canada together as a nation.

Nothing that came before or after can quite equal that.

There was nothing particularly idealistic about Wong-Tai's reason for being in the Canadian Rockies. He was there for the 75 cents a day.

And, similarly, it was money rather than any offhand "because they were there" concept that led men to the first determined assault on the high west wall of the prairies.

The determination was displayed by two famous competitors—The Hudson's Bay Company and the North West Company. Both sought to be the first to open a route to the Pacific and to control Canada's fur trade.

What saved the conquest of the Rockies from being just a cold, commercial chapter in Canadian history were the men the rival companies chose for the job.

These men were hardheaded and businesslike enough, all right.

But, as the quotation from David Thompson at the opening of this introduction shows, these men saw something much more than money in the mountains.

That is what made them, and men and women like them, the "Mountainmen" of our title.

* * *

ADVENTURERS

High on one flank of Mt. Eisenhower lies a sloping alpine meadow. There, 7,000 feet above sea level, a person can sit beside the deep cut of a mountain stream and look up the last 3,000 feet to the towering summit of the famous "castle" of the Rockies.

Those 3,000 feet symbolize a great deal of the adventure of the Rockies.

Few could sit in that meadow without imagining the thrill of standing on that summit. And fewer still could bring themsleves to the task of the fearful climb up that final, vertical cliff.

Every quarter hour or so the summer sun cracks rocks free from the cliff. The rocks fall for long, silent seconds before booming and exploding into dust along the scree of the foot of the cliff.

Only 3,000 feet, but in those 3,000 feet lies the essence of the sublime danger that has always drawn — and always will draw — the adventurer to the Canadian Rockies.

Sometimes the 3,000 feet are a real, vertical obstacle to be surmounted. Sometimes they symbolize what it takes for a man to face "just one more season" of hunting for a gold mine that probably exists only in legend.

Sometimes they are the magic lure that draws a man back to the mountains after a lifetime of violence and danger and killing work.

Each of these "sometimes" has a man, and a story, that goes with it...

* * *

"The old instinct to ride after buffalo again came over me, and I have to admit I always have a keen appetite for any kind of good strong drink..."

—GEORGE 'KOOTENAI' BROWN

* * *

George Brown was a man who couldn't have existed outside the era of the opening of the Canadian west. And possibly that era couldn't have existed without George Brown.

He started out as a quick-triggered soldier of fortune and ended his days as an irritable old civil servant arguing with Ottawa about lost fire pails.

He was a law unto himself, and even that law was made only to be broken. Tall, powerful and fast, he went through life afflicted with the kind of temper that draws guns and sometimes pulls triggers.

His genteel British accent never managed to hide a tongue so rough that those who knew him said he invented a new curse every time he opened his mouth.

In later years, he wore his pale blonde hair hanging to his shoulders; some say in imitation of his friend Buffalo Bill, but perhaps it was only a wistful effort to cling to a fading era.

Poisoner of wolves, slaughterer of buffalo, gambler, Indian fighter, whisky trader — George 'Kootenai' Brown was all these things.

But he was also a man with a vision, a vision that led his life out in a long, looping circle from the Rockies and, in the end, brought him back to the Rockies again.

It was his determined following of that vision that redeemed him and that lets us remember him as one of our great mountain pioneers.

It was 1865 when George Brown first set foot in what is now Alberta. His education was behind him — Eton and Oxford — and so was the finishing school of a soldier's life in Panama and the life of a drifter in the western United States.

Behind him, too, was the darkest incident of his life. In Montana a fight had flared across a poker table and he had killed a man. No one, today, knows just what happened.

Brown himself kept the incident a secret and, although there is some evidence he was arrested for the shooting, there is no evidence he was ever brought to trial.

Probably the closest Brown ever came to talking about the incident was once, in his old age, when he told a friend that the sweetest words in the English language are "Not Guilty."

Whatever happened, he had headed north after the incident, lost himself in the gold fields of the Cariboo.

Now, two years later, he and four companions were riding down the east slope of the South Kootenai Pass and out onto the open prairie. They were bound for Edmonton where they had heard there was gold to be found.

As Brown recalled later, "We had no very clear knowledge of where Edmonton was, and there was no one to tell us."

Brown was convinced that the party should stick close to the mountains and head north, but his companions didn't agree. Reluctantly he followed their directions, and he almost didn't live to regret it.

Unknowingly, the party's looping route carried them into the heart of Blackfoot country.

At that time, the Blackfoot nation was at the peak of its power. Still uncrippled by white man's diseases, white man's whiskey and white man's bullets, the Blackfoot in 1865 were one of the fiercest and most efficient fighting forces in history.

Apart from Brown's party, there probably weren't more than a few white men in all Alberta at the time. And, learning from the experiences of tribes to the south, the

Blackfoot were anxious to see even these few white invaders driven out of their lands.

Years later, Brown remembered that trouble wasn't long in coming:

"One day, at a clump of cottonwood trees, we stopped to eat. Well, as we were eating we were suddenly surprised by a flight of arrows from the direction of the cottonwood trees and we knew that our first war party had begun.

"We all thought our time had come. The Indians had no firearms, but they were all young bucks, 32 of them, no old men or war women. All young warriors. A war party out for anything they could get. They had lots of arrows and they let them fly.

"We got up and started shooting at anything we could see. We had not much cover, only some brush, and the Indians had driven us away from the cottonwoods, many of which were two feet in diameter. If the Indians had guns they would have killed all five of us.

"It was at this time I received an arrow in the back, close to my kidneys. It was a miracle I was not killed—I thought my time had come—but I pulled it out, an arrow head two and a half inches long and the head out of sight. The jagged edges caught the flesh as I pulled it out, and it gave me great pain.

"I had a bottle of turpentine and, opening up the wound, one of my companions inserted the neck of the bottle and when I bent over about half a pint ran into the opening made by the arrow head. This was all the doctoring I ever got and in a few days I was well again.

"We were using old muzzle loaders with balls and caps and we carried bullets in our pockets and in our mouths. Two Indians fell victims to our intermittent fire and the rest, after about 20 minutes fighting, rode to the river and jumping

their horses into the stream, swam them across, taking one of my horses and another with them…"

Brown, in agony with the arrow wound, didn't take long to lose his famous temper. The result was what he later described as a "miniature civil war."

When the dust finally settled, the party had split up. Three of the men pushed on along their original route. Brown never heard of them again.

The fourth man, whose horse had been lost in the Indian raid, reluctantly decided to stay with Brown. No doubt the man, noting the fact that Brown still had two horses left, hoped that Brown would give him one. But Brown had all his worldly goods packed on the second animal and wasn't about to part with it under any circumstances.

Instead, he "helped" his companion by building him a bull boat (a circle of willow covered with a green buffalo hide), packing him into it with a load of raw buffalo meat, and shoving him off from the bank of the Saskatchewan River.

Brown's casual explanation of the act years later was that *"I thought I might run across him at Fort Garry if the river flowed in that direction, but I was not sure."*

(For the record, the man did survive. Brown met him again some time later — though not, it should be added, at Fort Garry.)

Now on his own, Brown struck out towards Edmonton. Or so he thought. The problem was that he had convinced himself that the Saskatchewan River would serve as the highway to his destination. "I reasoned that it must flow into the Atlantic Ocean or Hudson's Bay and that it would eventually bring us to the fringe of civilization."

In fact, the river would bring him to Duck Lake and a new chapter in his life.

After several weeks of wandering along the twisting river,

Brown came upon a small band of Cree Indians. From them, he learned that there was a "A-pit-hou-a-goo-es san," a "village of half-sons," nearby.

The "half-sons" were the Metis, and the village the Cree referred to was a settlement of 50 families of hunters who were preparing to winter at Duck Lake.

Brown pressed on to the settlement and was immediately accepted by the hunters. He spent the fall and winter living as part of one of the families, sharing the tasks of caring for the valuable buffalo ponies and of hunting for food. By the time spring came, Brown spoke the language and had learned the intricate social pattern of Metis life.

He spent several years with the Metis people, taking a Metis girl as his "wife" and building a reputation as one of the best buffalo hunters in a society that knew no peers as buffalo hunters.

In his later years, Brown made it plain that he could happily have spent the rest of his life as one of the Metis people.

But, sadly, by the time he met them history was already closing in on their way of life. The Metis had joined in the frenzied extermination of the buffalo, and when the buffalo disappeared so did the nomad hunters.

Brown had drifted far from the mountains, and he would drift further still in distance, in time, and in feeling.

After he left the Metis, he joined in the life of the whiskey traders and wolfers who were streaming north across the International Boundary.

His recollections of this period are defiant, filled with a refusal to apologize for things of which he obviously felt deeply ashamed. One of Brown's anecdotes in particular catches the feeling of his life at the time.

Brown was engaged in the dubious pursuit of hunting wolves with poisoned bait, and on this particular day had

brought in a load of pelts to a trader named Johnnie Gibbons.

He arrived at the post to find it crowded with about 30 Red Lake Indians. Gibbons had only two clerks and he persuaded Brown to help in the post for the day.

"In those days," Brown explains, *"all traders sold rum and whiskey to the natives. Johnnie Gibbons was not any exception to the rule, and he put me in charge of dispensing the liquid. The Red Lakes would come in with a fur of some kind and hand it to me. It was my duty to give them as little whiskey as they would accept for it.*

"There were no bottles, cups, or glasses in use in the west at the time, but the Hudson's Bay Company brought in

thousands of little copper kettles and these soon came into common use.

It would be one of these kettles that an Indian would invariably push up to receive the whiskey in payment for his fur. Sometimes he would drink it where he stood and other times it was carried to his teepee.

"On this day the Red Lakes had run out of fur before their thirst for whiskey had been quenched. Chief Starving Wolf had come in and asked for a drink free gratis. By this time they were all very drunk and I didn't like to give them any more. So I said to him 'My friend and brother, you know I am not a man of two tongues. I'll give you one drink and that's the last you'll get.'

"So he drank his drink and left."

With the Indians gone, Gibbons sent an old man, Jimmie Clewitt, out to a storehouse behind the post to bring in a fresh jug of rum.

Brown was uneasy about the Indians and he was standing at the window. He saw Clewitt enter the storehouse and, an instant later, saw Chief Starving Wolf jump through the door after him, gun in hand.

"I yelled that the Indians had gone into the storehouse. Instantly we heard the report of a gun and saw Clewitt running for his life to the store. We also saw the Indian emerge with a large copper pot which we assumed was full of rum, and it was. Clewitt made for the house and falling into the porch groaned 'I'm done for'."

One of the post's clerks, Billy Salmon, had been concerned about the old man going out to the storehouse alone and had followed. He was with him when the shot was fired. Like the old man, he had made a run for the porch, collapsing in front of the door. He had been badly wounded and later died.

Brown continues: *"The Indians immediately began peppering away at the store from their hiding places behind the storehouse. Odd bullets came through the chinking and there was rattling and clashing of all sorts of stuff on the shelves. (We) grabbed muzzle loaders and whenever the leg or wing of an Indian appeared around the corner he was nailed. Even Clewitt, whom we expected was dead, jumped up and, grabbing a rifle, began peppering through a window.*

"After several rounds had been fired, an Indian jumped out from behind the storehouse, probably to get a good aim, and Clewitt and myself both shot him. Another Red Laker ran out to pull in his dead body, but while getting over a fence he was shot in the leg and fled, dragging the broken member after him."

The other clerk, in the meantime, had managed to sneak away from the post and run for reinforcements. Just as the men in the post were running out of ammunition, the clerk returned with a party of 20 half-breeds and whites. The Red Lakers fled.

The men in the post took time to tend the wounded Clewitt and to tidy up, then:

"I need hardly say that after this narrow escape every one of us got drunk, and while in that state someone — perhaps I did it — cut the head off the dead Indian and, climbing to the roof of the store, stuck it on a stake standing up through the thatching.

"There the head remained for many weeks, a most weird and gruesome sight with its long hair blowing in every breeze..."

For a few years, Brown's life was a jumble of incidents like this. Finally he could stand it no longer.

Years earlier, when he had first come through the South Kootenai Pass to the prairies he had paused at a chain of lakes, the Kootenai Lakes (later to be known as the

Waterton Lakes). At the time he had been struck by the beauty of the lakes and by the deep conviction that his place in life was on their shores. He vowed that someday he would return and make his home there.

Now, 12 years later, he remembered the vow. He was finally on his way back to the mountains and to the lakes that would make "Kootenai" his middle name.

Brown made a partner of a man named Fred Kanouse and the two opened a store on what later became Brown's homestead at Waterton.

The store attracted many Indian customers. Brown and Kanouse, despite the attraction of huge profits, avoided trading in whiskey. It wasn't a matter of morality. As Brown pointed out later they had both seen too many drunken Indians on the rampage to want to chance the consequences.

Despite the absence of whiskey, business boomed. It was as much a matter of gambling as good trading sense. Both Brown and Kanouse loved a bet, and they knew that Indians would gamble on just about anything.

Brown explains: *"Someone taught the Flatheads and Kootenais to play poker and this became their great pastime when they visited the store. It took a card shark to beat them. Kanouse was an expert poker-player so he attended to that part of the business.*

"I was a foot-racer and a good shot, and in competition on the track or with the rifle I could always beat them.

"We had two good horses and in horse-racing we always got the best of them. In fact, we beat them at every turn."

Being a consistent winner is not without its risks and Brown, in his memoirs, tells of one incident where the partners showed a decided flare for diplomacy.

"I have a very distinct recollection of one very interesting race, not on account of the race so much as because of the big stakes we put up.

"We had just sold the Kootenais $500 worth of goods for furs they had delivered. They asked for a race and we asked 'What stakes?.'

"They had no furs and no money but they had the goods they just bought. So they took these goods — saddles, bridles, lasso ropes, blankets, dress lengths the squaws had bought for gaudy gowns — and piled them up in front of the store.

"Then they rounded up 40 head of Indian ponies valued at about $20 apiece. They then asked what we would put up. Fred Kanouse had $500 in greenbacks and he told them we would put up this against their pile of goods and horses. And the race was on.

"Kanouse rode Honest John and the Indians had two or three horses in the field. Honest John won easily and we carried the goods in and put them on the shelves again.

"The bucks took the loss quite philosophically but the squaws put up a howl. They said to their lords and masters: 'You are fools. You let these white dogs swindle you. It will soon be winter and we have no clothes, blankets, or anything else.'

"There were only three white men of us ... and there must have been nearly 70 full blooded Indians. So we had to go slow.

"Kanouse suggested giving every squaw a blanket which we did, and every buck a knife or plug of tobbaco or some small trinket he might ask for.

We also gave back the poorest of the horses we won, for some of the poor beggars were on foot and would have to double deck or walk back to the Flathead country. But we kept the best of the horses and all the saddles, bridles and other goods.

Every man, woman and child got some little present and away they went back to their stamping grounds quite happy."

Brown's most famous gambling story, of course, concerned the acquisition of his second wife, Nichamoose. Brown, a widower at this point, saw the girl when a band of her people came to trade at the store and he decided he would have her as his wife — at any price.

The price her family demanded was five horses and Brown paid cheerfully — which should have made them suspicious. No sooner was the transaction complete than Brown lured them into a bet and ended up with his five horses back and a new wife to boot.

Gambling and diplomacy nothwithstanding, the store was a short-lived proposition for Brown and Kanouse. Most of the Indians who traded with them came from what was officially the United States side of the international line.

As the border stiffened, more and more of the Indians traded in the U.S.

Brown and Kanouse decided to close up shop. Kanouse bought out Brown's share of the goods and headed out to set up a general store in the town of Macleod. Brown stayed behind to homestead by the lakes he knew and loved.

Long before anyone else, Brown considered the Waterton Lakes area a national park. He became the area's protector, stamping out careless or abandoned campfires, doing what he could to control irresponsible hunting. When the area was finally made a national park, George 'Kootenai' Brown was named its first superintendent.

Brown was aging and — very reluctantly — settling down. He had two homesteads on the go, and he was coming

to uneasy grips with the bureaucracy of park administration. He had even made his marriage to Nichamoose legal, with the famous missionary, Father Lacombe, performing the ceremony.

Kootenai Brown was always enough of a visionary to know that civilization would come rushing into the west. But even he was bewildered by the speed with which what had been his way of life for so many years disappeared overnight.

It must have seemed ironic to him to write Ottawa for authority to control gambling among the tourists who were flocking to the park.

And for a man of the open range it must have taken a great deal of soul-searching to lead the way towards fencing off the ranch land around Pincher Creek. He did it only because, in the winter of 1911, 4,000 head of cattle had drifted into the park, and 2,000 head had died from cold and starvation.

In time, Brown would even have his famous, flowing hair cut. The job of park superintendent, he felt, demanded a certain dignity.

Brown was prepared to accept the need for civilization but, short hair or not, he just didn't have it in him to become a civilized man himself. Although he learned to control his temper, he never lost the wild, free feeling of the pioneer mountainman.

Perhaps no story sums up the older Kootenai Brown better than the one of how, in 1910, at an unmellowed 70 years of age, he took part in his last buffalo hunt.

Although the buffalo were basically exterminated during the era of the hide-hunter, a few did survive. These were eventually built into the famous Pablo herd (later to be moved to Wainwright).

It was the Pablo herd that gave Brown his chance at a final hunt.

"A bunch (of buffalo from the herd) got away to the mountains," Brown writes. "They belonged to Pablo and he got an idea that he would finish up the days of real buffalo hunting with a party of old-timers to go after these. He began looking over the country for a few real old buffalo hunters that were left.

"One day I got a letter delivered to me by a long lanky half-breed cow-puncher. It was a letter someone had written for Pablo inviting me to be present at a buffalo hunt for a week.

"The half-breed told me of the preparations Pablo was making and the amount of good whiskey he was putting in store.

"I couldn't resist the invitation. The old instinct to ride after buffalo again came over me, and I have to admit I always have a keen appetite for any kind of good strong drink. We are not getting nearly as good whiskey as we used to...

"Anyway I accepted the invitation of Pablo and I rode my old buck-skin over the border to Montana.

"The most distinguished guest was Buffalo Bill, and to him fell the honor of killing three of the remaining buffalo. He was a great hunter. I have heard his wife tell of contests where he beat his opponents by killing nearly double the number of buffalo they could kill in the same time.

"Pablo himself got two, I got one, and several others got one each. Pablo presented each of us with the hides we killed and with as much meat as we could pack home.

"It was a tame meeting compared to the days when we hunted herds of thousands of animals...

"I have never seen a buffalo since, either wild or in captivity."

Ten years later George Kootenai Brown was dead. His grave is on a high point overlooking the park that is his legacy.

There has never been another man quite like him — "either wild or in captivity."

* * *

"In the name of Almighty God, by Whose strength I have climbed here, I capture this peak, Mt. Robson, for my own country, and for the Alpine Club of Canada."

—REV. GEORGE B. KINNEY

* * *

When, in 1909, the bareheaded Rev. Kinney staked his claim to the roof of the Canadian Rockies, he was claiming it for more than country or club. He was also claiming it for the "grand old man" of Canadian mountaineering — Arthur O. Wheeler.

It was Wheeler who created Canada's Alpine Club, and it was Wheeler who stood, in spirit if not always in fact, with every Canadian pioneer climber on the peak of every Canadian mountain they conquered.

On so many trails in the Canadian Rockies there comes a point where mere mortals can go no farther, where the trail guide says "experienced climbers only" and means it.

Beyond that point is a whole world of towering cliffs and cornices, a world of ropes and ice-axes and pitons and climbing ladders; the world of Arthur Wheeler and men like him.

Wheeler came to mountaineering relatively late, at the age of 40, and he came to it more out of necessity than out of choice. A trained surveyor, Wheeler had been with the federal topographical surveys branch off and on since 1885, and was an expert in phototopography.

In 1900, assigned to help map the Canadian Rockies, he discovered that the only way he was going to get his camera equipment to the tops of the mountains was to carry it there, and he set to work on a crash course in mountaineering.

What started out as a labor of necessity, however, soon turned into a labor of love. Alone in the high, wild world of the Selkirk range, Wheeler discovered, like so many men before him, the place where he belonged.

By 1905, when he published his survey of the Selkirks, Wheeler was as thoroughly a man of the mountains as if he'd drawn his first breath there.

In fact, Wheeler was born to the comparative levelness of Kilkenny, Ireland, and lived there until his parents brought him to Canada at the age of 16.

Right from the time of his arrival Wheeler "burned" to explore the vast and largely untamed country in which he found himself. And, in 1876, the best avenue to exploration for a young immigrant boy was to become a surveyor.

Five years later, in 1881, Wheeler's apprenticeship was behind him and he had qualified as an Ontario Land Surveyor.

By 1885 he was in uniform with the Dominion Land Surveyors' Intelligence Corps and played a part in suppressing the Riel Rebellion.

By 1900, Wheeler's list of survey accomplishments stretched on an on: work on the CPR, settlement surveys for the North West Territories, summers alone in a birchbark canoe on the Great Lakes.

But then came the Selkirks and Wheeler's rendezvous with Alberta history.

If Wheeler had climbed out of the Selkirks in 1905 as just another man in love with the mountains, his name would be forgotten — or at best little known — today.

What he came out with, in fact, was an urgent vision. Alone, looking out over the sea of peaks, Wheeler had been struck by the realization that most of the mountains he saw had never been named, never been climbed. The Canadian Rockies were one of the last great frontiers of mountaineering.

Wheeler knew it was inevitable that all these mountains would soon be conquered, and he was determined that they would be conquered in the name of Canada.

In 1906, with the help of Mrs. H. J. Parker of the Manitoba Free Press and of Calgary's Rev. J. C. Herdman, he founded the Alpine Club of Canada. The next year he started the Canadian Alpine Journal and became its first editor.

Wheeler's Alpine Club quickly became the focal point for the efforts to conquer Canada's peaks. Climber after climber came to Wheeler for advice as they planned their assaults.

At some point in this period Wheeler seems to have made a decision about the role he would play in the campaign to claim Canada's mountains for Canada. Another man might have been tempted to make it a personal campaign, turn it into personal triumph, but Wheeler chose another course.

Although he continued to climb enthusiastically, and although he took part in many expeditions, he deliberately moved himself into the background. He became the man who organized, who encouraged, who applauded, but never the man who stood triumphant in the spotlight.

The decision has a curious effect on his story. Increasingly, his contribution to Canadian alpine history tended to blend into the stories of other men, and increasingly it is in these other stories that Wheeler is to be found.

One of the best illustrations of this is the story of the efforts to conquer Mt. Robson. In the early 1900's Mt. Robson, standing at 13,700 feet, was considered the highest mountain in the Canadian Rockies.

In 1906, shaping plans for the new alpine club, Wheeler suddenly realized that, though many had seen and passed the giant of the mountains, no one had actually attempted to climb it.

Wheeler immediately seized on the idea of an attack on Robson by Canadians as the most appropriate way to set the club on its way.

Ever enthusiastic and ever persuasive, Wheeler cornered the famous brothers of Canadian climbing, L.Q. Coleman and Prof. A. P. Coleman, and urged them to try the climb. By the winter of 1906, Wheeler had the Colemans convinced and they began making plans for an expedition the next summer.

In August, 1907, the Colemans were on their way to the mountain. At the last moment they had recruited a promising young climber, Rev. George Kinney, as the third member of their team.

One of the greatest difficulties the team faced, apart from the climb itself, was the problem of getting to the mountain. Mt. Robson stands west and north of Jasper and, in 1907, there was no Jasper Highway nor even a clear-cut passable route.

The Colemans and Kinney chose to go north from Laggan (Lake Louise). It was probably as good a way as any, but it wasn't good enough. It took them 41 days, weeks longer than they had expected, to reach the base of Robson.

They had one tantalizing glimpse of the peak, then storms moved in to shroud the mountain in clouds. The clouds and the storms stayed.

The party had arrived to late in the season and the frustrated trio finally had to return to civilization, without having gone any higher on Robson than the timberline.

The next year the three were back again, and again too late in the season to be sure of good climbing.

The too-familiar clouds were in place when they arrived, and they settled down to wait. Two days later the weather cleared. But two days later it was Sunday, and Rev. Kinney was quite emphatic about "no climbing on Sunday." The weather closed in again by Monday morning.

Five days later it cleared enough for the party to climb. The Colemans and Kinney made it to 10,000 feet, then were driven back by rain and darkness. Another day of storm and then the weather cleared. Sunday again. The Colemans must have been sorely tempted by atheism.

Snow moved in the next day and stayed for three weeks. The Colemans and Kinney tried to climb anyway, from time to time, but were always driven back by storms.

Finally, with the food supply nearly exhausted, they decided they had to admit defeat. But Kinney insisted on one final — solo — attempt on the mountain.

It took until nightfall to reach the 7,000 foot level and he spent the night shivering in a blanket, unable to light a fire.

At dawn he was climbing, inching his way up to 10,500 feet. Floundering in deep snow and pounded by a mounting gale that literally blew him off his feet on repeated occasions, he finally had to give up. Later he insisted he would have continued his attempt the next day if he hadn't promised the Colemans that he would be out only one night.

The next day, as the party was packing to leave for home, the weather cleared again and they decided on one last climb. They made it to within 1,200 feet of the summit but had to turn back, frustrated, when darkness closed in.

It was the end of another year. The three parted company, agreeing to meet in Edmonton for another attempt on Robson the next August.

The next May, however, Kinney heard rumors that a "party of foreigners" was on its way to attempt the elusive peak. He rushed into action, Determined to head off the foreign attempt, he hurried from his home in Victoria to Edmonton to stage his own assault.

In Edmonton he contacted John Yates, the packer who had been with the expedition the two previous years. But Yates refused to have anything to do with an attempt on Robson so early in the season. Spring had been late and the mountains were hidden under heavy snow — with the threat of avalanche increasing daily.

Kinney, however, had made up his mind to climb Robson and he was going to do it, Yates or no Yates.

On June 11 he set off alone, his three horses packed with provisions and with only a couple of dollars and some loose change in his pocket.

He wasn't particularly worried about being alone, having, as he explained later, vague hopes of meeting someone on the trail "who would share fortune with me."

He was deep in the Athabasca Valley, drying out after being stranded for several days by the flooding Rocky River, before he met the fortune-sharer he had been hoping for.

It was Donald (Curly) Phillips, who was later to become one of the more famous Rocky Mountain guides, but who was at this time on his first trip into the mountains.

Phillips had never climbed a mountain before, but the eager Kinney somehow persuaded him he could learn all about mountaineering — on Mt. Robson.

It wasn't until he stood, craning his neck back to try to see the top of the forbidding mountain, that Phillips realized what he had got himself into.

Curly Phillips, however, wasn't a man to back off from anything. So, tied behind Kinney with a length of ordinary rope, and with a piece of stick for a mountain axe, he set off to climb his first mountain.

In three days, with Kinney forced to cut ice-steps much of the way, the pair had made it to 11,000 feet. Yates, the packer, had been right about avalanches. They whistled by Kinney and Phillips with frightening regularity.

The pair retreated and brought up supplies to establish a camp at the 10,000 foot mark. Then Kinney cut steps up to the 12,000 foot point. There, however, the two were pummelled by falls of ice and stones and were forced to flee for their lives.

During the flight, Kinney noted later, "the now-melting snow masses that covered every ledge threatened to slide from under our weight and drag us over the cliffs.

"Phillips," he added wryly, "was fast becoming an expert in climbing."

They were forced all the way back to the base and had to wait out eight days of storms before they could climb again.

On the ninth day, at first light, they were hurrying up the mountain. On the west shoulder, at 10,500 feet, they dug through the snow covering a ledge, built a little wall of stones to keep themselves from rolling off the mountain, and settled down to shiver out the night.

Kinney and Phillips both knew that the next day would have to be their final attempt on the summit.

At dawn, stiff with cold, they started to climb again. The morning was clear but only briefly. Soon they were struggling up through clouds of sleet and mist. Kinney later said the conditions were "a blessing, in a way, for they shut out the view of the fearful depths below."

Hours later they were on the icecap of the summit, so surrounded by swirling snow that they could hardly see their hands in front of their faces.

Kinney swung his ice axe at the lip of snow in front of him and ... "it cut into my very feet, and through the little gap that I had made in the cornice, I was looking down a sheer wall of precipice that reached to the glacier at the foot of Berg Lake, thousands of feet below. I was on a needle peak that rose so abruptly that even cornices cannot build out very far from it.

"Baring my head, I said, 'In the name of Almighty God, by Whose strength I have climbed here, I capture this peak Mt. Robson for my own country, and for the Alpine Club of Canada'."

On their way back, just outside Jasper, they met the "foreigners" Kinney had been so anxious to beat. In fact, the "foreigners" were a collection of the most brilliant climbers in the world: Sir Edward Whymper, Arnold Mumm, Geoffrey Hastings and Leopold Amery — the last three of the British Alpine Club, and all four with conquests of more than 20,000 feet on their records.

The four British climbers heaped praise on Kinney,

writing later that "no mountaineering success was ever more richly deserved, or won by a finer exhibition of courage, skill and indomitable perseverance."

Kinney's triumph was complete — or so it seemed.

His fellows in the Canadian Alpine Club — particularly the sharp-eyed A. O. Wheeler — were the first to notice it. There was an elusive something wrong with Kinney's triumph, something vaguely dissatisfying in the way he talked of it.

Soon rumor was circulating even outside the clubrooms: Somehow, by accident, Kinney had turned back a few feet short of the summit of Mt. Robson. The mountain was still unclimbed.

Kinney denied the suggestion hotly. But suspicion nagged on, troubling Wheeler and a few of the other club members.

Some members felt the mountain should be climbed again to confirm the club's claim of its conquest. But they hesitated to do anything, however indirectly, that would suggest Kinney had been lying.

It was A. O. Wheeler, finally, who stepped in to do what had to be done. It had been his suggestion that had launched the Colemans and Kinney on their three-year struggle with Robson. He had brooded over their efforts, urged them on, encouraged them when frustration seemed to gain the upper hand.

He had cheered Kinney's triumph, and now he was prepared to do whatever was necessary to keep that triumph from turning hollow.

In the summer of 1813, under Wheeler's personal supervision, the Canadian Alpine Club set up camp at the base of Mt. Robson. Wheeler hand-picked the team for the assault: Albert MacCarthy and William Foster, two of Canada's best climbers, and Conrad Kain, indisputably the best alpine guide in Canadian mountain history. Wheeler spent hours with the team, plotting the best line to the summit.

The day came for the climb and the three moved out at dawn. Kain cut ice-steps at a furious rate, refusing to let up even for a moment. At some points the three had to wade through hip-deep snow.

Eight hours later they saw, just above them "great masses of ice and rock. dome upon dome, swept clear by raging storms to reveal clear green ice scintillating in the sun." And just above that was the summit.

A short while later, squeezed together on the slim, top-most spire of Mt. Robson, they cemented the Canadian Alpine Club's claim on the peak.

On their way back down, they noted the route Kinney and Phillips had taken in 1909.

Conrad Kain described it as "quite the most dangerous way that could be chosen up the peak" and insisted that Kinney and Phillips "deserve far more credit than we..."

Bit by bit, in the years that followed, the truth of what happened during Kinney's attempt on Robson came out.

The main information came from Curly Phillips who said that, climbing in the blinding storm, he and Kinney "had reached on our ascent an ice-dome 50 or 60 feet high, which we took for the peak. The danger was too great to ascend the dome."

It would be half a century before Kinney himself, now an elderly man, provided the final word. He conceded that he had probably been "mistaken" in his claim and had actually stopped a few feet short of the summit.

One wonders how Wheeler, if he had still been alive, would have felt to hear the wisdom of the decision he made in 1913 finally confirmed.

Firmly planted on a slope overlooking Banff, on the

site Wheeler picked for them, are the headquarters of the
Canadian Alpine Club. Wheeler designed the building and
personally supervised its construction.

It makes a fine landmark. The kind to guide the way
for all the other young boys who "burn" to be explorers.

* * *

"I've decided to give it maybe one more try..."

MIKE CZECH

* * *

It takes a few minutes for a visitor to realize that the
far-away gleam in Mike Czech's eye is the gleam of gold.

Sitting in his perpetually half-finished house in Coleman, Czech displays a talent for avoiding questions that
would do credit to a cabinet minister.

He has a habit of staring off into the distance and stirring
uneasily in his seat as though he wished the annoying
questions would go away — or as though he wishes he
were somewhere else.

When forced to answer, he is liable to say vaguely that:
*"Well, maybe I'll tell you about that one of these days. Why
don't you come back in..."*

All this becomes understandable when you realize that
Mike Czech is in the grips of that legendary, lost, cursed
gold mine: the Lost Lemon.

Czech is not an old man (somewhere in his 40's by
appearance, but even here he remains vague) but he has
devoted most of his adult life to the search for the mine.

It doesn't bother him that many have died on the same
quest. Or that all the evidence available suggests the mine
never existed, that it was all a grotesque hoax on the part
of the claim-seeder.

"It's there all right," Czech insists with a half-smile. He
will say no more.

"There" to Czech and to most of the others who spent
their lives searching for the mine, is the Livingstone Range,
that massive forbidding block of mountain stretching north
from the Crowsnest Pass almost to Rocky Mountain House.

The legend of the Lost Lemon is easily told.

In 1870 a party of prospectors came north from Montana to scour the North Saskatchewan River for gold.

With them were two men named Lemon and Black Jack who split away from the main party to search the Highwood River.

Working upstream they found traces of gold and followed the traces toward the headwaters.

Somewhere along the way they struck paydirt, rich diggings and a ledge that was the source of the gold.

(One supposed sample of the find made its way to Fort Benton in Montana where traders described it as "a body of solid gold with little rock shot in it.")

In camp the night of the find the partners quarrelled and Lemon, waiting until after his companion was asleep, split Black Jack's head open with an axe.

Thrown into a panic by realization of the enormity of his murderous act, Lemon built up the fire and spent the rest of the night pacing back and forth like a caged beast, rifle in hand.

His panic wasn't eased by the sound of ghastly moaning and twittering that filled the air around the camp.

Unknown to Lemon, the murder had been witnessed by two Stoney braves, William and Daniel Bendow. It was they who were providing the sound effects that were driving Lemon to terror and that sent him fleeing on horseback at first light.

Fearful that news of a gold find would draw an army of prospectors into their hunting grounds, the Stoney chief Bearspaw swore the two braves to secrecy when they told him what they had seen.

Lemon made it back to Tobacco Plains in Montana. There he confessed the murder to a priest who was an old friend of his, and he showed the priest a bag of the gold he said he and Black Jack had found the day of the crime.

The priest sent another man, John MacDougall, to the scene of crime. MacDougall buried Black Jack and piled stones over the grave to keep off wolves and to act as a landmark.

As soon as MacDougall left, the Stoneys tore down the cairn and scattered all traces of the grave and the camp.

All winter Lemon remained with the priest, hovering always on the edge of insanity.

By spring, however, he was apparently well and, with the organization of the priest, led a large party of miners north to find the mine.

Lemon, however, was unable to find the site. After days of searching, the miners became convinced Lemon was trying to mislead them, keep them from the gold.

They threatened Lemon with death and he promptly became violently insane. Although he would have lucid periods from time to time, he remained insane for the rest of his life.

The miners had to turn back.

The next spring another expedition, again organized by the priest, set out. The guide was to be MacDougall, the man who had buried Black Jack.

But on his way to join the search party, MacDougall stopped at the whiskey post of Fort Pitt and drank himself to death. Again a hunt for the mine had to be called off.

Every year another party would set out and every year fate — or tragedy — would frustrate it.

The most notable hunter was a man named Lafayette French who claimed to have a map drawn by Lemon.

For 15 years he scoured the hills in search of the mine. One night, in the early 1890's, French sat down and wrote an excited letter to a friend at Fort Benton. He had, the letter said, finally found "IT."

Later that night the cabin burned to the ground.

French escaped, but so badly burned he couldn't speak before he died.

Searchers later found, melted in the ruins of French's cabin, what was rumored to be "thousands of dollars" worth of gold.

With French's death, the search for the Lost Lemon lost most of its steam. Also, there was the growing conviction that the mine was guarded by an Indian curse. .

And from time to time there would be found in the range the remains of cabins with food, rusted rifles, cooking kits, rat-eaten bedrolls. Men don't abandon these things in the wilderness — unless tragedy strikes.

Gradually the hunt for the mine became the mission of "foolhardy" men like Mike Czech. And finally it has become the mission of Mike Czech himself.

So much for the legend. But what are the facts?

Late in the 1960s, Glenbow historian Hugh Dempsey probed the legend and took it apart piece by piece.

He found Black Jack was a real man and a well-known prospector — the only problem, in terms of the legend, being that he was alive and in a hospital in Victoria 13 years after he was supposedly murdered by Lemon.

Lemon's friend the priest was identified in early accounts as Father LeRoux. Church records showed no priest of that name ever served in the area.

But Dempsey found the LeRoux of the legend suspiciously like a French-Candian adventurer named Jean L'Heureux, particularly since the names LeRoux and L'Heureux are identical in sound.

L'Heureux had studied for the priesthood but, after a

scandal, fled to the Montana gold fields where he posed as a priest and missionary.

In 1862, he was connected with a gold-seeding scheme which sent an expedition of miners rushing north to Fort Edmonton.

Dempsey asks if it is "mere coincidence" that a phoney priese named L'Heureux started a false gold hunt in 1862 and that a mysterious priest named Father LaRoux sent out search parties in search of the Lost Lemon in 1871?

The matter of Lafayette French's gold is also cleared up.

It turns out the gold was discovered in the cabin years after French's death — and that it had been planted there by its finder as part of a cover story to explain some gold illegally smuggled in from the United States.

The Stoney braves, the Bendow brothers, who witnessed the murder of Black Jack also proved a shaky part of the legend: The name Bendow appears on no treaty lists and Stoneys, questioned later, said they had never heard of the existence of the name in their tribe.

Finally, there is Lemon himself. Dempsey found an American prospector named Frank Lemon who, on an expedition into "Lost Lemon" territory, had lost his partner — known as Old George — in a shooting. Whether he was shot by Indians or in a quarrel with Lemon was never explained.

Lemon also claimed to have found gold on the trip — not a jackpot but a good showing that "got as high as $15 or $20 in the pan in a gulch."

The find, it turned out, wasn't even on the same side of the mountains as the supposed Lost Lemon.

Add to this grim little tale the meddling of the adventurer L'Heureux and the legend takes shape. And becomes no more than legend.

Still, Senator Dan Riley — who knew French, and L'Heureux both — continued to finance searches for the mine right up to the time of his death.

And the Stoneys, to this day, remain determinedly silent on the subject of the Lost Lemon and refuse to assist in the hunt for it — for reasons that have never been given.

The Lost Lemon. The name is well-chosen since lemons are gold — and bitter.

But Mike Czech, despite discouraging years of searching, is convinced the mine is there to find.

In the end, what difference does it make if the mine exists or not?

Mountainmen have followed more futile dreams into a place in the history of the Canadian Rockies.

EXPLORERS

"I thought we were not keeping close enough to the mountains."

— GEORGE 'KOOTENAI' BROWN

* * *

It took more than half a century for the white man to find a "road" through the Canadian Rockies.

For the men who took part in the search, it was an exercise in frustration. After all, it is one thing to be searching for something you only "think" is there. It is quite another to be searching for something you "know" is there.

And the early explorers "knew" the road they sought through the mountains existed; the Indians of the Canadian Rockies were using it — or, as it turned out, "them" — all the time.

For a number of reasons, Indians were determined that the explorers and traders weren't going to find any easy way through the mountains.

For the Indians, it was a last chance to retain control of part of their shrinking world.

It was also a matter, in the case of the Peigan Indians for example, of keeping enemy tribes deep in the mountain interior from getting their hands on guns that traders would provide.

It was one of the longer and more successful conspiracies in the history of Indian-white relations, and it wasn't without its humorous side.

Traders and explorers were often able to persuade Indians to guide them to one of the mysterious routes, but somehow these searches always ended up in a blind canyon or at the foot of a cliff, with the Indian guide scratching his head in feigned perplexity.

Not the kind of thing to improve the temper of an impatient explorer.

Of all the men who set out in search of the elusive road to the western sea, four names stand out above the others: Alexander Mackenzie, Simon Fraser, David Thompson and Sir George Simpson.

Alexander Mackenzie, in his expedition of 1793, wasn't really out to find an "easy" road to the Pacific. His was basically a scouting trip, to spy out land for a fur trade that was running short of fur east of the mountains.

But his push into the interior of the Rockies laid much vital groundwork for the two explorers who would follow him.

And perhaps Sir George Simpson, that crusty baron of the fur business, shouldn't be on the list at all.

Except that when the road was finally found he painted one of the most flamboyant white lines in history right down the middle of it.

* * *

"The judge had a nephew in need of an occupation; the North West Company was in need of sturdy young clerks who seemed to have talents…"

—FROM AN INTRODUCTION
TO THE JOURNALS OF SIMON FRASER.

* * *

Simon Fraser has been described as the most neglected of Canada's major explorers. As one historian notes, even the majority of his journals and letters have been published in forms that were "without exception inaccurate."

With the help of his uncle-judge, Fraser was apprenticed to the North West Company at the age of 16.

That was in 1792. From that time until he emerged in his famous expeditions that ended with the conquest of the Fraser River in 1808, he remains an historic enigma.

Almost nothing is known of his career.

There were at least four Frasers with the North West Company at the same time and Simon Fraser's name stands out with certainty in the company records only once.

That was in 1801 when a unamimous vote made him a partner, with a 46th share in the profits of the Nor'westers.

If nothing else, that acceptance to partnership at the early age of 25 demonstrated that Fraser had become a man the company valued.

Fraser's concern as a partner was the operation of North West's Athabasca Department and it led him directly to his assignment as the company's mountain explorer.

By the early 1800s, both the North West Company and The Hudson's Bay Company were suffering from over-extended supply routes.

The fierce competition between the companies was pushing trade farther and farther west as Indians over-trapped in efforts to meet the demands of the rivals.

By the time of Fraser's acceptance as a partner, the forests east of the Rockies were virtually trapped out and the companies were both operating deep into the mountain interior.

The North West Company was suffering most from the move westward.

The Hudson's Bay Company was bringing in supplies and shipping out furs through its ports on Hudson Bay and James Bay — no short trip, but certainly shorter than that of the Nor'westers who had to ship back and forth between the Rockies and Montreal.

The Nor'wester line was simply too long to stand the strain. The answer was a route through the mountains to the Pacific and Simon Fraser was given the job of finding it.

What made the task of Fraser and the other fur company explorers particularly difficult was that the road they were seeking had to be one made out of water. A portage here and there was acceptable, but with the loads made up in bundles of 90 pounds — and the usual assignment of two bundles to a man — a dry route was out of the question.

The Nor'westers were particularly intrigued by the Columbia River. They knew it came out at the Pacific, and Mackenzie's explorations in 1793 had created the belief (mistaken) that he had found the upper reaches of the Columbia.

So, in 1805, Simon Fraser was instructed by his company to advance up the Peace River, cross the Rockies, establish trading posts in what is now the interior of British Columbia, and endeavor to trace the Columbia River to its mouth.

Those instructions resulted in two expeditions, the last in 1808 finally taking Fraser and his men down the river that would later bear his name, a river that even today is described as "one of the most difficult and dangerous in the world."

That final journey was, in terms of what he had set out to do, a failure. The river hadn't been the Columbia. And it hadn't by any stretch of the imagination turned out to be a river that would serve as a trade route through the Rockies.

Still, even in his own day and even among the men in the North West Company who suffered most by the failure, Fraser's journey was considered a triumph of human courage and endurance.

And the very enormity of what he had done set the stage for those who would follow, those who would finally find the watery road to the sea.

History is always particularly good at describing the ends of things — the disaster of final failure, the triumph of victory over great obstacles.

But what about the beginnings of things?

In Fraser's case, the tale of his final terrible trip to the sea has been told many times and in many ways.

More important, in his rough, impatiently written journal, he does what few men remember to do: he records how it began.

And that story, of the first stage of the first journey, is every bit as exciting as the final tale of the thrust to the sea.

Fraser received his instructions in the summer of 1805 and by the fall of that year he had led a party of 20 men up the Peace River to the foot of the turbulent Peace River Canyon.

There he established a base camp and, being a good businessman, he also established a trading post.

All winter, waiting impatiently for spring break-up, he and his men restlessly expanded outward from that first trading post to gain firm control of fur trade in the district.

Two men in Fraser's party stand out particularly — though in distinctly different ways.

The first was his second-in-command, John Stuart, who would be at Fraser's side on all three of his journeys of exploration. It was often Stuart, as the excerpts that follow from Fraser's journal show, who kept the expedition — and its men — alive.

The second man was probably one of the most aptly named men in Canadian history: La Malice.

La Malice was Fraser's senior voyageur, and time and time again he lived up to his name with displays of incredibly shifty, mean and unreliable behavior.

By late spring in 1806, Fraser was ready to begin and La Malice wasn't the only problem he faced in making that beginning.

John Stuart was Fraser's only capable canoe-maker and Stuart was much to busy with other duties during the early spring to devote much time to the work.

The result was that Fraser was left to begin the journey in three canoes that were ill-made and in constant need of repair.

Worse yet, the men he had available were a sorry lot, largely incompetent and in ill-health.

A typical birchbark canoe of the type Fraser used needed a crew of three: a bowman, a steersman and a middle man. The most important man in each canoe was the steersman. And, as Fraser would note with dismay in his journal, none of his steersmen were any good.

Fraser himself took charge of the first canoe, Stuart of the second and, to the eternal woe of all concerned, La Malice became the fourth man in the third.

We pick up Fraser's journal on the first day of the journey.*

WEDNESDAY, MAY 21: *"About sunset Mr. Stuart and I took our departure with two canoes, and encamped at the first point. La Malice will follow tomorrow as soon as the canoe will be arranged. Mr. Stuart's canoe made a great deal of water, and is so rude and ill-made that they were every moment in danger of over-setting it, for which reason we will be obliged to pass a couple of days at this place to arrange it. It is the worst-made that ever I saw and is more like a trough than a canoe ... It would be more easy to make a new one than to arrange it."*

FRIDAY, MAY 23: *"Fine warm weather. A strong head wind all day. At noon we were obliged to put ashore to gum (gum from evergreen trees was used to seal leaks in the fragile bark canoes), the canoes being so leaky that we could not prevent the property from getting wet. Here we lost four hours ... Little Gervais, who steers Mr. Stuart's canoe, is not able to keep it straight. Indeed, the want of a steersman will greatly retard our progress up this strong current."*

*Some editing, to correct spelling and replace archaic or unclear words, has been done in these excerpts. Certain deletions have also been made for reasons of space.

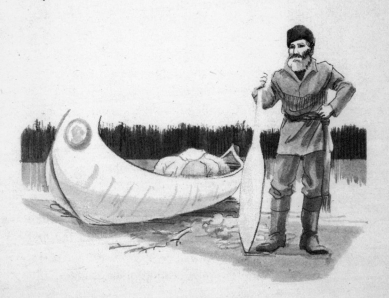

SUNDAY, MAY 25: "*Set off early, and soon after came to the foot of the strongest rapid we saw yet. The canoes were towed up with the line but one of them struck upon a stem which broke a small hole in the bottom and it took us near an hour to repair it.*"

TUESDAY, MAY 27: "*...the water rises very fast. Indeed it has risen upwards of three feet since we left ... We came to and encamped at the last rapid ... La Malice, who was before us, attempted to ascend this rapid with the pole, but Mr. Stuart, who was the nearest to him, called to him to desist ... It was really difficult to come up this rapid, and we were obliged to take out the load and carry it over a rocky point of 400 yards, and the canoes were taken up light (paddled up unloaded). La Malice, who was first up, left his canoe with only the bow of it on shore, and while he was busy at the lower end it went off and ran down the rapid ... they went for it with another canoe. I was much displeased with La Malice on this occasion, as well as with his attempting to go up with a full load, and threatened him severely if he was not more careful in the future.*"

WEDNESDAY, MAY 28: (At this point, Fraser's party, still following Mackenzie's route, has turned east to follow the Parsnip River) "*... which is overflown, and the current was so very strong that it was with much difficulty we could advance. No use can be made of the poles on account of the depth of the water, excepting some times against the banks and drift wood, and the current runs with such velocity that it cannot be stemmed with three paddles, and not easily with four ... and the banks are so thickly interwoven with trees and shrubs that it is seldom they can be approached, so there is no method left except that of going up by pulling the branches, and the canoes are in*"

*continual danger of being broke to pieces by the drift
wood."*

THURSDAY, MAY 29: *"The water still rising and wood con-
tinually drifting down the river. My canoe was very near
cut in two."*

FRIDAY, MAY 30: *"We set off at half past 4 a.m. ... a stump
(a few hours later) ran through my canoe, which obliged
us to push ashore, and we lost two hours ... We encountered more misery today than any day yet, and were obliged
to cut several logs and obstructions to open a passage.
My canoe through the awkwardness of the bowman and
steersman was very much endangered and every soul on
board near perishing."*

MONDAY, JUNE 2: (The expedition this day reaches the lake
that is today identified on the map as McLeod Lake.)
*"Here we left one of the canoes and separated its load
on the other two, on account of all the men being nearly
exhausted with fatigue, and especially La Garde, who
steered my canoe since the 26th of last month, has such
a sore wrist that he is no more able to."*

TUESDAY, JUNE 3: (The party is once again moving but
is brought up short about noon.) *"Both canoes have
become so heavy and shattered that they cannot be taken
out of the water by less than four men."*

(Finally, on June 8, the party reaches Fort McLeod, one
of the posts which Fraser had established earlier. There
Stuart and La Malice supervise the construction of two
new canoes, the old ones now being beyond repair. It
isn't until June 23 that the expedition is able to move
on along the Nechako River. Two days later, the expedition is once again in difficulty — though of a different
sort.)

WEDNESDAY, JUNE 25: *"La Malice paddled only at intervals*

today, he being unwell, and in the evening he declared himself disabled ... What ever it is, he appears to suffer very much and is quite disabled. It is really vexing..."

FRIDAY, JUNE 27: "...we went on well, but was obliged to put ashore on account of La Malice, where we lost four hours. As he could not sleep for several nights past, last night Mr. Stuart gave him 30 drops laudnum, and he complains of being worse since ... La Malice seems very weak and often delirious, and yet he eats as well as the others."

SATURDAY, JUNE 28: "We were not above half an hour gone when La Malice jumped on shore, we being near the bank, and fell down senseless. This obliged us to put ashore and pitch our tents for the night ... By all appearances, if he (La Malice) is really as bad as he pretends, he will not live long. We are all really ill off in regard to the men. Saucier is sick, Gagnon complains of his side, Blais of having a pain and a lump upon his stomach, and Gervaise is not well, and La Londe is not able to steer his canoe."

SUNDAY, JUNE 29: "About noon we were obliged to put ashore and light a fire to warm La Malice and cook for him. He will eat nothing but cakes and pemmican boiled up with flour and sweetened with sugar."

TUESDAY, JULY 1: (La Malice, complaining of being treated like a dog in his illness, claims Fraser and Stuart have a grudge against him. News of this reaches Fraser.) "This assertion of his, La Malice, is entirely false. We have been attentive and kind to him ... and nothwithstanding his complaints he used more than one half of the medicines (God knows good or bad)we possessed, and destroyed more flour and sugar than both of us did since we left ... I recollect when St. Pierre (one of the men) fell in a fit *he was abandoned by La Malice, and scarcely drawn out of the water, and when I afterwards reprimanded him for his apparent disregard of his duty as a Christian, even if he was indifferent to the feelings of humanity, he told me laughing that as he thought he (St. Pierre) was dying, he left him to die alone, and set about mending his canoe, but now it is his turn to suffer and he complains."*

THURSDAY, JULY 3: (The two canoes are now on the James River.) *"Our progress will be very slow now, as we will be continuously compelled to put the people of both canoes in one on account of the current and rapids being too strong to be managed by four men, and none of them adroit. The navigation of the river is very dangerous on account of it being narrow, the current running so swift and many trees and obstructions laid across."*

FRIDAY, JULY 4: *"We set off early, with both canoes ... and through the awkwardness of the men mine was run against a large obstruction in the middle of the river, which broke the bow and smashed all the pieces to the second bar (rib). all hands jumped out and pulled the wreck on shore before it had time to fill and sink. We lost the most part of the day to mend it ... This labor always falls to Mr. Stuart's lot, there being no other person that can do it."*

MONDAY, JULY 7: *"Gave all hands a dram to cheer up their spirits after their violent exertion during the whole day. All hands worked hard and Mr. Stuart and my share of the labor is the most difficult, as we not only work in the canoes the same as the others, but are obliged either one or the other to examine the river on foot before we risk the canoes, so that as soon as we arrive with the canoe at the place we return from on foot, we embark again to examine farther on."*

WEDNESDAY, JULY 9: *"All the goods are entirely wet and*

the provisions are spoiling. When we arrived at this place the canoes were no more able to float, their bottoms being entirely hashed, and after getting bark and gathering some gum we patched them up for the present. The weather was cloudy all day and towards the evening it rained."

THURSDAY, JULY 10: *"Fine weather. After the canoes were gummed a little we continued on and had better going than we had reason to expect ... At 10 a.m. we arrived at the large river, opposite an island, without encountering any other difficulty than cutting several trees that laid across the channel ... This is a fine river..."*

Fraser thought he was finally on the upper reaches of the Columbia. Instead, he was on the river that would later be given his name. And it would be two years before he discovered it wasn't such a "fine river" at all, even if it did — finally — take him to the sea.

Sixteen days later, on July 26, the first stage of Fraser's expedition ended.

During those 16 days, Fraser had to cope with a guide who, as it turned out, didn't know where he was going. He had to cope with starvation as supplies ran out and game and fish became elusive.

He even had to cope with the mauling of one of his voyageurs by a bear.

The first stage ended at what is now called Stuart Lake. There — in a frustrating illustration of just how desperately long the Nor'wester supply line had become — he had to wait until the fall of the next year for supplies and fresh men.

What the first part of Fraser's journal shows, the part that appears in fragments here, is something of the incredible hardships that had to be faced by the men who set out to conquer the Rockies.

The image left of Fraser himself is much the same as

that of the river he conquered — an image that commands respect.

Although he had his detractors, not even his most severe critic ever called him unfair, dishonest, or without honor.

Indeed, the character sketch written by Fraser-scholar E.O.S. Scholefield in 1908 probably best sums up the "most neglected" of our Mountainmen:

"...a well-built active man, with heavy, almost dour, face, whose distinguishing features are a determined chin, firm, large-lipped mouth, prominent somewhat snubbed nose, light-blue eyes, broad receding brow, overhung with a mass of tousled hair of reddish tinge — a strong, honest face, indeed, but one giving more the idea of determination and physical robustness than of intellectuality or refinement.

"A man inured to hardship; versed in woodcraft and the lore of the savage; strong in danger; of inconquerable will and energy; unlettered, not polished, it may be, but true to his friends and honourable in his dealings; somewhat eccentric if we judge aright; a man typical of his age and calling.

"An heroic spirit truly, if case in the not altogether heroic mould of a fur-trader.

"He stands there a commanding figure."

* * *

From the ocean they expected a more boundless view, a something beyond power of their senses which they could not describe..."

—DAVID THOMPSON ON HIS MEN'S FIRST REACTION
TO THE PACIFIC.

* * *

News that Simon Fraser's river had turned out to be neither the Columbia — nor navigable — frustrated the North West Company, as had other explorations before.

For two years, they let the project of the route to the Pacific sit.

Then, late in 1810, came news of a development that made finding the route imperative. American traders, under the leadership of John Jacob Astor, had landed at the mouth of the Columbia River and built a fort and trading post.

Unless something was done quickly, the Indian fur trade that had been coming east through the Rockies would reverse direction and go to the Americans waiting in the west.

For one Nor'wester at least, there was no question of what had to be done.

"Everything was changed," he noted in his journal when he heard the news of Astor. "I was now obliged to take four canoes and to proceed to the mouth of the Columbia to oppose them. Accordingly, I set off from Lac la Pluie."

The man who made that note was David Thompson, and his determination was about to put the second "sea" in Canada's "sea to sea."

In 1810, Thompson was nearly 30 years old, and his career had reached the point where he could well afford to rest on his laurels.

He had come to Canada at 14, apprenticed to the Hudson's Bay Company. Later, he had moved to the competition, the Nor'wester, and now like Fraser he was a partner in the company.

By training and by instinct, Thompson was a shrewd and gifted trader. But he was gifted in a far more important way as well: As a surveyor and map-maker.

It was only by accident that this second gift was ever discovered — accident in more ways than one. In his late teens, while still with the Hudson's Bay Company, Thompson suffered a very bad fracture of his right leg. The injury left him an invalid for more than a year.

In the winter of 1789-90, towards the end of this period

of recovery, he encountered a man named Philip Turnor, the chief surveyor for the Hudson's Bay Company. Turnor and Thompson were stranded together in Cumberland House for most of the winter.

To pass the time, Turnor taught the youth the rudiments of geography and astronomy. David Thompson proved to be an exceptional student.

By the time winter was over, he was skilled in mathematics, astromony, and field surveying. He knew the survey use of the compass, the telescope, the thermometer and chronometer. He had learned to use the Nautical Almanak, the sextant and the artificial horizon.

From that point on, David Thompson would be as much explorer as he was trader and, during the next 22 years of his life, he would personally survey and map almost two million square miles of Canadian wilderness.

To understand what he accomplished, one has to realize that before he started the entire map of western Canada was blank. When he finished, it was filled.

In 1810, when he set off to oust Astor from the mouth of the Columbia, Thompson was only two years from retiring from the west and, by standards of his day, far too old and tired for so difficult a mission.

And the mission was far more difficult than even Thompson could imagine. While there are many passes in the Canadian Rockies, there are only four real breaches in the 1,000-mile wall. And only one of these, the Peace River route, has what the early traders were looking for: a waterway that pierces the entire mountain chain.

Thompson knew nothing of the Peace route. He did know, however, that many rivers had been followed from the Pacific far up into the mountains. It was the link with the same river that had eluded Fraser that Thompson was determined to find — the link with the Columbia.

Thompson knew he had no reason to be optimistic of finding it. Three times before — in 1800, 1801 and 1806 — he had set off on the same search, and three times he had failed. And he had watched the stubborn and capable Simon Fraser fail as well.

Thompson, however, was not a man to accept failure.

In November, 1810, he set off from Rocky Mountain House with a party of men. Heavily burdened with supplies and trade goods, the party spent four weeks hacking through thick bush as it pushed northward towards the Athabasca River, which Thompson believed to be the first link in the chain to the Pacific.

When the party emerged from the timber onto the flats and marshland near the Athabasca, the going got easier, but away from the protection of the trees the men felt the full impact of the winter cold. It was a steady 30 degrees below zero. The punishing cold drained strength away, left the men bitterly weary and clumsy.

Thompson's party was immobilized for days, the men barely able to muster the energy needed to hunt for the game they needed to supplement their food supplies.

It was the end of December before they were finally able to push on, following the Athabasca into the mountains. Most of the party's pack horses were too weak to carry a load, so supplies were transferred to improvised dog sleds. With game scarce and supplies running low, Thompson had to slaughter several of the horses for food.

He had to send some of his men back to Rocky Mountain House. A few others deserted. Thompson made the rest continue against their will.

By the end of the first week of January the party was just south of the present site of Jasper and almost hopelessly bogged down in deep snow.

Thompson was forced to lighten the sleds and to leave

a large quantity of supplies cached under the care of one of the party. The few remaining horses were exhausted and Thompson turned them loose. The men added the horses' loads to what they were already carrying on their backs.

With 13 men and 8 dogsleds left, Thompson pushed on 15 more miles south along the Athabasca valley to the juncture of the Whirlpool River. Thompson decided to turn to follow the frozen Whirlpool.

Toiling up the 5,000-foot climb, Thompson couldn't know he had finally found the key to what men had been seeking for half a century: a road to the Pacific.

Nor could he know that the route he was pioneering would open up the whole inland range—the last frontier of the fur trade—to eager Hudson's Bay men and Nor'westers.

On the night of January 10, the party was camped on an icefield, high in the mountains. Thompson was worried and restless. For the previous few days the weather had been bad; snow and mist making it impossible to judge where they were or the condition of the country around them. Tonight, finally, the weather had cleared and Thompson left the circle for an anxious, solitary walk.

It was an exceptionally clear night, and Thompson soon pulled up short. For the first time he saw where he was: on the western edge of a deep cut through the mountains.

Far below him, curving off the the southwest, was a river that looked vaguely familiar. If the river was the one he knew as the Kootenae ... He forced the exciting idea from his mind and returned to camp.

Thompson had been right, however. The river was the Kootenae, and soon it and a network of small waterways were leading the party westward until finally, on January 26, Thompson reached the shore of the Columbia River.

The days from the 10th to the 26th of January, however, had been costly ones for Thompson.

Most of his men were voyageurs, used to canoes and rivers. They were superstitious, and frankly terrified by the strangeness and loneliness of the mountains.

In his journal, Thompson mentioned one instance of this superstition and terror — an instance that reminds one of the legend of the Sasquatch:

"Strange to say," Thompson wrote, *"here is a strong belief that the haunt of the mammoth is about this defile. I questioned several of the men. None could positively say they had seen him, but their belief I found firm and not to be shaken.*

"I remarked to them that such an enormous heavy animal must leave indelible marks of his feet and his feeding. This they all acknowledged, and that they had never seen any marks of him and therefore could show me none.

"All I could say did not shake their belief in his existence."

Thompson might have wanted to treat this display of superstition lightly, but he couldn't. He had too-vivid evidence that this fear was combining in the worst way with the effects of weeks of physical hardship.

He was losing men steadily; some because he had to send them back for supplies, but more from simple desertion.

The real crisis came on the morning of January 26, the day he was finally to reach the Columbia. Thompson decided he had to send three of his remaining eight men back to pick up stores that had been cached on the trail. They had hardly left when four other men deserted. Of his original party of 13, Thompson now had only one man left.

Together they pushed on the last few miles to the Columbia. But here Thompson's luck seems to have gone astray.

He didn't realize the river was the Columbia. He guessed again — wrongly this time — that he was on the Kootenae.

Although he was impatient to push on, Thompson realized he had no choice but to wait here until he had supplies and reinforcements and — most importantly — some kind of boat.

With the help of his companion, Thompson constructed a rude cabin by the river and settled down to wait.

It was more than a month before reinforcements arrived: three voyageurs, an Indian guide, and two dogsleds of trade goods and dried provisions.

Thompson immediately set his party to work on the problem of a boat, only to find that birchbark, the usual material, wasn't going to work. Birch in this location was too thin-skinned for canoe construction.

"We had to turn our thoughts to some other material,"

he writes, "and cedar wood being the lightest and most pliable for a canoe, we split out thin boards of cedar wood of about six inches in breadth and builded a canoe of twenty-five feet in length by fifty inches in breadth, of the same form of a common canoe, using cedar boards instead of birch rind, which proved to be equally light and much stronger than birch rind.

"The greatest difficulty we had was sewing the boards to each round the timbers. And we had no nails, we had to make use of the fine roots of the pine."

It was mid-April before Thompson was ready to continue his trip. By this time, however, he had decided his party was still too small and too low on provisions and trade goods (these to bribe whatever hostile Indians they might meet). So Thompson led his men off towards the Nor'wester posts already established in what are now the states of Montana and Washington.

The detour lasted nearly three months, with Thompson dividing his time between rebuilding his party and practising diplomacy among the Indians of the interior.

It was July 3 before Thompson was once more on the Columbia (and aware of it this time) and on the stretch-run to the Pacific.

On July 10 he met Indians who had encountered the Astor party and he saw seals playing in the river. On July 15, Thompson finally saw the Pacific itself.

Thompson notes the sighting in his journal as "a great pleasure," but he adds wryly that: *"my men seemed disappointed. They had been accustomed to the boundless horizon of the great lakes of Canada and their high rolling waves.*

"From the ocean they expected a more boundless view, a something beyond the power of their senses which they could not describe; and my informing them that directly

*opposite to us, at the distance of five thousand miles, was
the empire of Japan added nothing to their ideas…"*

Late on the morning of July 15, the astonished men
of Astor's post looked out across the water in time to see
history bearing down on them.

*"We saw a large canoe with a flag displayed at her stern
rounding the point we called Tongue Point,"* one of the Astor
men wrote later. *"The flag she bore was the British, and
her crew was composed of eight Canadian boatmen or voyageurs. A well-dressed man, who appeared to be the
commander, was the first to leap ashore…"*

* * *

A FEW YEARS LATER

"At a season when the water was very high, one of the
Company's boats was descending the river; and, through
the rashness of an American who happened to be on board,
the crew were induced to run this rapid, while the gentleman in charge more prudently resolved to prefer the
portage.

"Hurled madly along by the boiling waters, the boat
was just emerging into a place of safety, when she was
sucked, stern foremost, into a whirlpool; and, in a single
instant, a tide, that told no tales, was foaming over the
spot where eleven men, a woman, and a child, had found
a watery grave."

The above account of an accident on the Columbia River
is from the records of The Hudson's Bay Company. The
accident occurred about 15 years after Thompson's discovery of the road to the sea and it shows just how unsafe
that road would always be.

* * *

"As we had more of the sun in the boat than on horseback,

*three baths a day were scarcely sufficient to make the heat
endurable...*"

—Sir George Simpson

* * *

The three men who did most to conquer the Rockies
— Mackenzie, Fraser and Thompson — were all from the
North West Company.

It is one of the ironies of Western Canadian history that,
in the end, it was The Hudson's Bay Company — the
Nor'westers arch rival — that reaped the benefits of the
conquest.

In the years that followed Thompson's journey to the
mouth of the Columbia, Hudson's Bay men poured into
the Rockies. Everywhere the Nor'westers turned, they
found Bay men opposing them.

It was a bitter struggle for control and the Nor'westers
were the weaker side.

The Hudson's Bay Company had made powerful allies
— including the same Jacob Astor that Thompson had been
sent to the Pacific to oust. The combined wealth of Astor
and Bay was too much to withstand.

The struggle went on for 10 years, finally ending with the absorbtion of the North West Company by its rival.

During those 10 years, Bay men and Nor'westers wrestled, and often fought, over control of the mountain trade.

Wherever the post of one company went up the post of the other was soon facing it. Indeed, in one case, the rivals shared a common stockade.

Violence was common. So were arson and theft. Even the Indians — torn between the two companies and perhaps inspired by their tactics — became increasingly hostile.

To add the violence of man against man to an environment where man already faced a desperate day-to-day struggle for survival was tragic.

The surrender of the Nor'westers in 1821 ended the battles of the traders. It also brought into prominence a man named George Simpson, who soon would earn himself the title of the "Little Emperor" of the fur trade.

Simpson (later Sir George Simpson) was given control of the Hudson's Bay Company a year before the Nor'westers surrender and it was Simpson who shaped the final campaign that resulted in that surrender.

Following the take-over, Simpson hurled back and forth through the Bay holdings in the west, showing a ruthless capacity for organization and an equally ruthless firmness in bringing an end to the violence that still lingered in the mountains.

Elegantly dressed, linen stock at throat and personal piper leading the way, Simpson would march into a camp of hostile Indians and immediately humble them — or browbeat them — into an agreement of peace.

Just how badly that peace was needed is shown by an extract from Simpson's own journals, an extract that comes from a time long after "tranquility" had supposedly returned to the Rockies.

"At Okanagan," he writes, "we were concerned to learn that the Indians of the interior, as far back as New Caledonia, principally the Schouschwaps, were in a state of considerable excitement. The cause was as follows.

"In the month of February last, a chief of the name of Kootlepat visited Mr. Black, the gentleman in charge of Thompson's River, at this post of Kamloops, when a trivial dispute took place between them.

"Immediately on returning to his camp, at a place called the Pavilion, Kootlepat sickened and died, enjoining his people with his last breath to keep on good terms with the whites.

"Whether or not the chief's dying injunction was interpreted into an insinuation that he had perished in consequence of having quarrelled with his white brother, the Indians came to the conclusion that Kootlepat's death had been caused by Mr. Black's magic or medicine.

"In pursuance of this idea, the widow of the deceased worked upon the feelings of her nephew, till he undertook to revenge her husband's untimely fate.

"The avenger of the blood forthwith set out for Kamloops; and, when he arrived, both cold and hungry, he was by the orders of his destined victim, placed before a good fire and supplied with food.

"During the whole day, Mr. Black, who was a hard student, remained writing in his own apartment; but, having gone out towards evening, he was returning through the room where his guest was sitting, and had just reached the door of his chamber when he fell down dead, with the contents of the savage's gun in his back.

"In the appalling confusion that ensued, the murderer was allowed to escape from the fort, betaking himself immediately to the mountains.

"He was chased from place to place like a wild beast, being obliged to abandon first his horses and lastly his wife and family; but it was not till after eight months of vigilant pursuit, that he was finally hunted down on the banks of Fraser's River by some of his own people.

"As a proof of his comparative estimate of civilization and barbarism, this miserable being, with the blood of Mr. Black on his conscience, earnestly begged to be delivered up to the whites; and on being refused this last boon, he leaped into the stream, swimming away for his life, till he was despatched, just like a sea otter, by arrow after arrow..."

Such incidents were common, and common, too was the way this one had started in suspicion and distrust.

But it is significant to note that it was the slayer's own people who pursued him and executed him. The influence of the Little Emperor was already showing.

By 1841, the empire of The Hudson's Bay Company stretched around the world, with outposts in the south seas, the Orient and Russia.

Simpson, as the organizing genius behind the empire, decided it was time to make his own mark as a conqueror of the mountains and set out to find his own route through the Rockies to the mouth of the Columbia.

It was to be part of a spectacular dash around the world, with Simpson visiting every part of the international trade empire of which he was governor.

His journal of that global voyage fills two volumes and the section dealing with the trip between Fort Edmonton and the Pacific has close to 70 pages to itself.

Despite his discovery of the pass that today bears his name, Simpson's journey through the mountains doesn't really stand out as a key event in the exploration of the mountains.

It does stand out, though, as an example of how much the style of exploration had changed since Thompson's day — particularly the style of an explorer who had the resources that went with being governor of one of the world's great trading monopolies.

Simpson was not a patient man. He didn't like to dally when he travelled and his organizational demands rode down all obstacles to speed.

By sending out advance parties to await him with fresh horses and with boats, and by travelling with the best party of packers and guides and boatmen in the company, he was able to average 40 to 50 miles a day where Tomppson and others had been lucky to make 10 or 15 miles a day.

Simpson habitually had his party moving by three or four in the morning and thought nothing of "getting a start on the day" by having them race 20 or 30 miles before breakfast, ending the race by having them carry him ashore from the boat to his meal.

But then, a few short excerpts from his journal can sum up the man and his journey better than the words of another:

". . . *Leaving our old band of horses under the charge of the Indians, we immediately started with thirty-two fresh steeds. After crossing a prairie of two or three miles in length, we spent two hours in ascending a steep mountain, from whose summit we gained an extensive view of ranges of rocky hills; and, while the shadows of evening had already fallen on the valley at our feet, the rays of the setting sun were still tinging the highest peaks with a golden hue.*

"*We encamped at the foot of the mountain with wolfish appetites, for, though we had a good deal of exercise during the day, yet we had eaten nothing since seven in the morning; but what was our disappointment to find that six horses — one of them, as a matter of course, being the commissariat steed — were missing!*

"*Having exhausted our patience, we went supperless to bed about midnight; but hardly had we turned in, when a distant shout made us turn out again in better spirits.*

"*The horses quickly arrived; and before an hour had*

elapsed, we had despatched a very tolerable allowance of venison-steaks and buffalo tongues."

Elsewhere, Simpson describes another meal, this one drawn from the supplies of one of the company posts along his route:

"Just fancy, at the base of the Rocky Mountains, a roasted turkey, a suckling pig, new bread, fresh butter, eggs, ale, &c.; and then contrast all these dainties with short allowance of pemmican and water.

"No wonder that some of our party ate more than was good for them..."

Whatever else he did, the Little Emperor set a style for mountain travel that would later be echoed in the linen, crystal and silver of dining cars, and he created a demand for speed that only the coming of the trains could meet.

After Sir George Simpson, the Rockies would never seem the same again...

*   *   *

AN EXPLORATION FOOTNOTE — ON THE LIGHTER SIDE.
*"He nursed a great desire to be attacked by a vampire, simply
so he could be in a position to say it had happened to him."*
—KEN LIDDELL

* * *

Nothing could be less like the man for whom they were named than Alberta's Waterton Lakes.

Whatever the season the Lakes area is always predictably serene. Charles Waterton was never predictably anything — least of all serene.

As a consequence, though he never even set foot in the province, Waterton has managed to win himself a place in Alberta history as our most "oddball" explorer.

The son of an English squire, Waterton was a naturalist, and a good one. Indeed, it was his reputation as a naturalist that led a member of the Palliser expedition to name the lakes for him.

Unfortunately, Waterton's professional reputation was often obscured by his bizarre techniques.

Very few scientists other than Waterton, for example, ever chose to capture a full-grown boa constrictor by the simple expedient of knocking it out with a right hook to the jaw.

Nor have many other scientists let their curiosity lead them to a ride on the back of an alligator. Waterton did this, vaulting onto the napping alligator and twisting its forelegs up behind its back to use as a bridle.

He chose never to repeat the twisting, bucketing experiment because, as he explained, he had found the seat decidedly "uncomfortable."

Waterton built a wall, ten feet high and three miles long, around his English home. Within the wall he created a sanctuary for buzzards, crows and magpies because, he contended, these birds were victims of discrimination.

Even outside the scientific community, Waterton had the reputation of being ... well ... slightly unusual.

He never wore shoes outdoors, even when tramping through the jungles of South America.

At home, he slept on the bare wooden floor.

And he greeted friends by growling and biting them affectionately on the ankle.

On one occasion, in Rome, after a wild reunion with an old schoolmate, Waterton was sighted perched on one foot on the head of a marble angel — a hundred feet up the face of a building.

When it came to personal health, Waterton was very much an advocate on the do-it-yourself approach.

On the rare occasions when he fell ill, or when he had an unfortunate encounter with a wild animal, Waterton's response was to dose himself with "laudanum, calomel, jalep and bark," and to draw from his arm "twenty-seven ounces of blood."

Since he lived to a ripe 83 years of age, it is hard to fault this otherwise dubious approach to medical science.

Although he did make one trip to Canada, Waterton never came as far west as the lakes named for him. Which, from his performance in the east, was probably just as well.

Spraining his ankle while jumping down from a train, Waterton remembered that one cured a sprain by pumping cold water over it. The pump which happened to be handiest at the time was Niagara Falls.

"I descended the winding staircase and hobbled to the scene of the action," he wrote later. "As I held my leg under the falls I tried to meditate on the immense difference there was betwixt a house pump and this tremendous cascade of nature, and what effect it might have upon the sprain; but the magnitude of the subject was too over-whelming and I was obliged to drop it."

In the end, Waterton's eccentricity has outlived his reputation as a scientist. His works are lost and his grave hidden by weeds.

All that is left is a collection of anecdotes and a string of peaceful lakes; lakes far too calm for the memory of so uncalm a man.

* * *

TAMERS

"On the mountaintops we stand, all the world at our command..."

—GORDON LIGHTFOOT

* * *

For more than 40 years after Sir George Simpson's flat-out race through the Rockies, a kind of stillness settled over the mountains.

Traders and Indians came and went in the routine traffic of fur trade. An occasional, unusually adventurous hunter would make the arduous trek west in search of big game.

But, somehow, the Rockies had become only a nice place to visit — and the trip was too much trouble to make the visit worthwhile.

All that changed with the coming of the railway.

This book is not the place for the great — and lengthy — story of the building of the CPR. That subject is dealt with well, and at due length, in other books.

But with the driving of the last spike in 1885, Donald Smith was also hammering home the first nail in the settlement of Alberta's mountain region.

Even before the last spike was in, William Van Horne

had renamed Siding 29 "Banff" and engaged an American architect to design for the mountain setting a hotel he could advertise as "the Finest Hotel on the North American Continent."

The hotel was designed to resemble a French chateau, in tribute to the French-Canadian voyageurs who had quietly contributed so much to the conquest of the Rockies.

At other sidings small chalets sprung up to accommodate passengers on the CPR's transcontinental trains.

Van Horne launched a massive advertising campaign, lauding the Rockies as "the Mountain Playground of the World," a description in use even today.

Van Horne's objective, of course, was to create passengers for the company's trains. And like the company's similarly-motivated campaign to bring settlers to the prairies, it worked and worked well.

A growing stream of people came to the Rockies. Some came to hunt or fish or climb. Some came for the healing powers of the hot springs in the Banff region (an area made a national park at the urging of the CPR). Some came simply for the peace and quiet and the clarity of the mountain air.

Around the railroad, and around the business of providing service to the visitors, sprang up a host of companies to supply food and supplies, guides for would-be climbers, carriages and horses for leisurely touring.

The people who provided the service built and often stayed to make their homes in the Rockies.

One of the first of note was an Irishman named John Brewster who saw the hot springs of Sulphur Mountain and anticipated the tourist boom that would follow the railway west.

Others, like Bill Peyto and Jim Simpson, were guides and packers who found tourism turning their trades into small industries, and who settled down to let civilization sneak up on them.

And there was one lady who settled down simply to paint ... and a churchman who wrote books ... and a man who strung a clothesline to a mountain...

There was nothing ordinary about the settlers of the Canadian Rockies.

* * *

"Most people are hemmed in by clocks and timetables and their molehills become mountains. The first time they see a real mountain they put the molehill in its proper place."

—JOHN BREWSTER.

* * *

Probably no single family has played a greater part in settlement — and development — of the Alberta part of the Rockies than the Brewster family.

Since the day John Brewster set foot in the mountains in 1887, the family's interests have grown to include Banff's Mount Royal Hotel, the Columbia Icefield Chalet and a string of motels and lodges that stretches from far north on the Alaska Highway south to the U.S. border.

Then there is the Brewster Transport Co. operating bus and taxi service throughout the Rockies. And Brewster Pack Trains Ltd. And the Kananaskis dude ranch and Devil's Head ranch.

Within a year of coming to Banff, John Brewster — a blacksmith by trade — had rounded up a herd of wild cows and was operating a milk route to the new Banff Springs Hotel.

His two oldest sons, Bill and Jim (Jim was six then) took care of the actual delivery.

Six years later the two older Brewster boys were in business on their own, at the ages of 12 and 11.

"Tourist attention!" their advertisement read, "Complete camping and packing outfits and experienced guides to any part of the Rocky Mountains Furnished on short notice at reasonable rates! Special facilities offered to fishing parties. W. & J. Brewster — Guides and Packers."

By that time the boys' father had taken a loan urged

on him by CPR and was well-established in the livery business.

In time there would be six Brewster sons, all actively involved in some aspect of the family business.

Of them all, perhaps the best-known was Jim Brewster.

By the time he was seven, Jim as an experienced horseman, hunter and guide, and he could speak Cree as well as he spoke English.

Like all the family, he developed a shrewd business sense. But in him it was mixed with a flair for adventure and showmanship that was to make him famous.

In 1904, at the age of 22, he and a friend duplicated the exploits of the early explorers and travelled the Columbia River in a canoe.

The next year he was leading one of the major hunting expeditions of the era, guiding a party to the Arctic to hunt muskox.

A tireless booster of the mountains, he travelled extensively in Europe and the United States to promote the Canadian Rockies. In time he became a friend of royalty and, in the process, a special protector of the remittance men who were banished to the anonymity of the Rockies.

"He showed them the mountains," one observer writes; "He showed them the game on which they could vent their spite; and if necessary he could drink them under the nearest icecap.

Another person who knew the young Jim Brewster writes of seeing him in town buying supplies for a hunting party — six loaves of bread and four bottles of whiskey. Asked what he was doing, he replied he'd just bought the supplies for the week.

"But what," asked the friend, "do you want with all that bread?"

Anecdotes tended to grow up around Jim Brewster.

Like the time he stalled the schedule of visiting royalty by detouring the king and queen of England by his house to meet his wife.

"I may forget a lot of things about the royal visit," he chortled later, but never my wife's face as we walked in the door. She was so excited she nearly fainted, and her face was as white as a sheet.

"However, it wasn't two minutes till the Queen and she were chatting away like old friends."

And when Brewster wasn't providing the ingredients for stories, he was telling them.

One of his stories, in particular, sums up the quality of his tale-telling.

In England in 1907 to promote travel in the Rockies, Brewster looked up an earl he had met in Canada and was invited to visit the earl's estate.

Brewster accepted and went off to catch the train.

"I had a crock with me and got into a first-class compartment. The train stopped once and the guard came to see me. 'As you are his lordship's guest, I just wanted to see you were all right,' he said.

"At the local station there was a car for me and another for my bag, and when I got to the castle a butler came to the door and said, 'I will anounce you to his lordship,' or some such twaddle.

"When I got in the hall, there was a line of flunkies with sideburns and I went into a room like St. Paul's Cathedral to meet his lordship.

"We got on fine, but the effect of the crock was beginning to wear off and we had some port. Now, I'm only used to California port, and this tasted like satin, and I maybe thought it was harmless.

"Anyway, when I got upstairs into a bedroom that looked like Grand Central Station without the steam heat, I couldn't find my clothes.

"The bag had been emptied and I thought I'd probably brought it down empty.

"Then there was a tent on the bed and steps up to it.

"When I began to get desperate, a valet came in and I tried to make friends with him, but it was no good.

"He held my pants for me to step into, and I found somebody had provided me with a tuxedo."

The next morning, Brewster found that someone had also provided him with a suit of hunting pinks and that he was off to the hunt.

"I was a real comedian, with a top hat and a red coat, a horse seventeen hands high, and three flunkies to help me up.

"The saddle had no pommel, and that worried me for a bit, but soon I got the hang of it.

"The dogs started to bark and I made the first fence all right, and that horse was the finest horse I ever knew.

"I passed the Duke of Beaufort, who was the Master of the Hunt, and then I passed the whips, who look after the dogs.

"I passed the hounds without stepping on any of them, and we were getting on fine when the thing was called off and a fresh lot of flunkies appeared with fresh horses.

"They loaded me onto another horse, and after a time I found the saddle bag had flasks of whiskey in them and we spent a fine afternoon…"

Jim Brewster went on through the years, telling stories and doing business and watching the communities of Banff and Jasper and Lake Louise grow and grow.

In later years he would lament a little that people no longer knew him on the street, and make the slight admission to age that the rear sight of his rifle looked "a bit feathery."

Jim Brewster and the rest of the Brewster family opened the wilderness of the Rockies to everyone.

And, thanks to them, no one is likely ever to mistake the mountains for molehills again.

* * *

"I may not be able to write, but, by George, I can preach!"
—C. W. GORDON

* * *

It was the summer of 1917, near the end of a terrible war, and there were few tourists among the crowd that streamed out of Banff one Sunday to the foot of Mt. Rundle.

There, on a rock by a lake known — appropriately enough as The Devil's Cauldron, a stocky dark-haired man in kilt and service jacket stood and began speaking.

He bagan hesitantly enough, as he always did, but as time passed his voice and words gained strength.

Rev. C. W. Gordon had just come back from the war in Europe. He had seen most of the men of his regiment perish in the horror that was France. At Somme, he had said the funeral rites for his colonel and friend.

In all truth, many of those who had come to the foot of Mt. Rundle that day hadn't come to hear the strong, solemn words of this preacher. In all truth, to many of the people before him, Rev. C. W. Gordon wasn't even C. W. Gordon; he was the most famous Canadian writer of the day: Ralph Connor.

So popular were his books that it was estimated at the time that one of every sixty Canadians had a copy of the famous "The Man from Glengarry."

In all, the novels he wrote sold a total of five million copies.

Even today, most people are familiar with such titles as The Sky Pilot, Glengarry School Days and Black Rock.

What those who listened to him that day at The Devil's Cauldron couldn't know was that the man facing them, the best and most successful Canadian writer of his day, was dead broke, ruined by the illegal acts of those he had left in trust of his wealth while he was away to war.

He said nothing of that in the sermon he preached. Instead he spoke of temperance, of courage and, above all, of forgiveness.

And, as was his habit, he spoke at great length. Those with Sunday roasts at home in the oven shifted uneasily before the vision of good roast beef shrivelling to charred leather.

Though much of his life was spent away from the mountains of Canada, Gordon was considered one of Banff's own sons.

What made this man, born in a small eastern town, a man of the Rockies? And what, even stranger, turned a committed missionary and minister into a popular novelist?

Gordon was born in Glengarry County in what was then Upper Canada in 1860, the same year his Presbyterian-minister father came to Canada from the Highlands of Scotland to escape the confines of the established Church of Scotland.

The father was a fearsome, evangelical preacher and his influence on his son was enormous. The younger Gordon never gave serious thought to any other way of life than that of a churchman — despite the fact that his father's exhortations to the good life were often accompanied by the banshee wailing of a bagpipe with which he used to shake the walls of the house for hours on end.

Gordon was later to admit that he spent his life intensely disliking the instrument and would flee at the very thought of it being played.

Little is known of Gordon's relationship with his mother, but it is significant to note that he said the gentle, long-suffering heroines of his novels were all based on her.

The boy was taught to work for everything. Even as a child of ten he hired himself out as a laborer and he worked his way through the University of Toronto, paying every cent of his tuition and expenses from his own pocket.

He spent some time at the university after graduating, teaching classics, then put himself through Knox College Divinity School and through two years at Edinburgh University in Scotland.

He was ordained as a minister in 1890 and called to missionary service in the Northwest Territories.

His first mission parish was Banff and he immediately fell in love with the mountain community.

Banff, in the 1890s, was far from being the pleasant tourist and resort town it is today. Rather it was a tough, hard-boozing settlement with more than its share of troublemakers.

A perfect town, as Gordon later noted tongue-in-cheek, "for an Evangelist."

A single man of 30, particularly one of such unquestionably sterling character, was an unusual attraction in a frontier town and Gordon was quickly drawn into the modest social life of the settlement.

Every evening, in one home or another, the young people of the settlement gathered to sing around a piano or to chat and sip tea. Gordon was one of the more faithful at these gatherings and, until recently, there were still old-timers in Banff who could recall that he would occasionally sing, in a fine tenor, for these parties.

Unfortunately, the old-timers pointed out, he usually accompanied himself on a guitar which he played exceptionally badly.

Ah well, a man can't be single, moral, a good singer and a good musician all at the same time. The girls of Banff took him to their hearts anyway and it looked for a long time as though he would find a bride among them.

But Gordon finally left Banff still a bachelor and it wasn't until he was 45 that a young Winnipeg girl, Helen King, won his heart and became his wife. He and Helen had six daughters and a son, King, who became a Rhodes Scholar and later an active figure in the United Nations.

In his long career with the church, Gordon would go on to become head of the Presbyterian Church in Canada and one of the leaders in the fight against booze, prostitution and conscription.

All this became overshadowed, however, by the emergence of his alter-ego.

Gordon was 36 and he had just made a futile trip to

Toronto to try to get church officials to raise money for missionary work in the west.

He had come away empty-handed but with an incidental set of instructions from the editor of the church's weekly magazine to write a story "to illustrate the need" of mission work in the west.

At the time Gordon was the over-worked minister of a run-down church on the outskirts of Winnipeg. Night after night, after prayer-meeting had ended, Gordon would go home and toil at the task of coming up with the required story.

The result, published first in 1896, was called Christmas Eve in a Lumber Camp.

The story was a fictionalized sermon about how a Presbyterian minister moved a camp of hard-drinking lumbermen to prayer.

Its name would later be changed to Black Rock and become one of the main stories in the first anthology of Ralph Connor's work.

The first story behind him, Gordon began to write and write and write still more. Being a fiction writer was not a respectable occupation for a minister so he was asked to come up with a pen-name. There was a sheet of mission letterhead on his desk when the request came and he compressed the first syllables in two of its words to come up with Cannor.

The publisher read Cannor as Connor and added Ralph because it seemed to go with the name. And so Ralph Connor — a non-existent being whom Gordon would later say had grown to become a "second person inside me" — was casually born.

Ralph Connor was prolific, his books came out at a rate of one a year, and wildly popular.

By the time his second novel appeared public curiousity over his real identity had reached a fever pitch and Gordon came — briefly — from behind the mask.

Much of the clamor for his true identity came in the United States where his work was so popular that it was made part of many high school reading lists. "The world will insist on knowing it," the St. Louis Democrat editorialized in its plea for the true identity of the author.

Connor's work is "so intense that one grinds his teeth lest his sinews snap ere the strain is released," The Chicago Tribune added.

And "his passionate writing appeals to all that is best in human nature," summed up the San Francisco Chronicle.

His identity out in the open, Gordon made lecture tours and, in the U.S., police had to be called out to hold back the crowds that gathered to hear and see him. President Woodrow Wilson was a well-publicized fan of Ralph Connor. And Henry Ford collected a complete set of autographed volumes of Ralph Connor's work.

In Detroit, when Gordon was asked to deliver a sermon

in a church, he rose to begin a prayer and the congregation spontaneously broke in with the singing of "For He's a Jolly Good Fellow."

Few men could stand so startling a thrust into fame and fortune without changing. In Gordon's case, it is to his tribute that all the fuss did was heighten his affection for the simple life and increase his sense of humor.

His New York publisher once described a visit to Gordon. He arrived at the house to find Connor was out.

"I was guided through a trail in the woods," he recalled, "to where he stood, bareheaded and alone, in sweater and old clothes, whittling a cane from roots of trees."

Carving canes — walking sticks — from the roots of trees was one of Gordon's ways of staying in physical touch with nature. So were riding a horse and paddling a canoe.

"I should have been born an Indian," he once lamented.

As for his sense of humor, a long-time friend once wrote that: *"He could unbend more completely than any man of his age that I have known."*

His favorite practical joke was one he reserved for the first time a new guest sat down to the Gordon's dinner table.

The guest would be placed at the end of the table, opposite his host, and at a signal from Gordon the people on either side would lift the oilcloth table covering to form a trough down which Gordon would solemnly pour his drinking water and then howl with laughter as the astonished guest received the watery cargo right in the lap.

After the guest was wrung out, fed and installed in the drawing room, Gordon would entertain him by an evening of singing as badly as he could while accompanying himself on a banjo he proudly claimed he could play worse than anyone he knew.

In fact, though, despite the recollection of his early

inability on the guitar, Gordon was an accomplished musician who could perform on the guitar, banjo or flute. Late in life he enhanced a natural singing voice by taking lessons.

He became so fussy on the subject of vocalizing that he thought nothing of stopping his congregation in mid-hymn to demonstrate how they could be singing better than they were.

By the time the First World War appeared on the horizon, Gordon's writing had made him a millionare. He had built a large home for his family in Winnipeg and a summer home in the resort community of Kenora, Ontario.

When Canada entered the war he went overseas as a chaplain.

A careful man, he left his financial affairs in order before he left. There was a $100,000 insurance policy and all his cash assets were turned over to a lawyer-associate to invest in the booming Winnipeg real-estate market.

The real-estate boom never materialized and the market collapsed in 1915, but Gordon was assured by his friend that his money had been protected and was divided among eight land companies the lawyer had set up.

It was only with the death of the lawyer, while Gordon was still overseas, that it was learned that the money had been misused and that Gordon had been left virtually penniless.

Connor's publisher recalled that it was almost impossible to convince him that he had been the victim of a criminal; and that, when he was finally convinced, his decision was to forgive the act and to do everything in his power to have it forgotten.

Nor did he allow the loss of his wealth to influence a life-long habit of open-handed charity. He gave everything he could to those in need during the depression years that followed the war, even though he was often as badly off as those he aided.

His financial disaster, however, seemed to open the door to a host of other troubles. Although he would go on writing and writing, in retrospect, better than he ever had before, his work began to lose its popularity.

Unable to recover from the loss of his money, he gradually had to give up the life-insurance policy he had hoped would provide for his family after his death. The same was true of the taxes on his homes and these too had to be given up, finally.

The only thing that never failed was Gordon's determined Christianity. He worked on and on, creating hostels for the homeless, acting as an advocate for the working poor.

But all that was still ahead, unknown to any of those who sat on the grassy slope by The Devil's Cauldron and listened to Canada's most famous author and best-known churchman.

This man, after all, was a brave minister who had gone to a terrible war to ease the misery of their sons and brothers and husbands. That made him part of them all.

And this man, too, was Ralph Connor: the author who had thrilled them with his adventures and fanned their courage with the examples of the firm-hearted characters he created.

When all is said and done, what they felt, sitting on the grass by a mountain lake, was right. There were two men before them.

It is the same judgement that history wrote on his gravestone when he died in 1937:

GORDON AND CONNOR
MINISTER OF GOSPEL

AUTHOR CANADIAN

* * *

"He just loved that mountain and that view so much he wanted to share it with everyone."
—RECOLLECTION OF A FRIEND OF JOHN JAEGGI.

* * *

Mountain tops are usually the private reserve of the special few who have the courage and the strength to climb to them.

In the Canadian Rockies, however, there is one mountain top that belongs to everyone, thanks to a Swiss-born guide named John Jaeggi.

Many of the thousands of visitors to the Rockies every year ride the gondola lift to the top of Sulphur Mountain to gaze out across the roof of Canada's mountain world.

The lift is almost taken for granted. So is the teahouse

on the summit. So, for that matter, is a bronze plaque outside the teahouse that few bother to read.

John Jaeggi came to Canada in 1924 and went to work as a guide for the Canadian Alpine Club. In his work, he became familiar with most of the peaks of the Rockies and, for some reason never fully explained he became enchanted with Sulphur Mountain.

It was a rather curious enchantment. Sitting too close to the edge of the Banff townsite to attract particular attention from mountaineers, Sulphur had been notable, until Jaeggi entered the picture, only as the source of the sulphur springs whose hot waters were one of Banff's tourist attractions.

As years went by and John Jaeggi expanded from guide to outfitter and packer he kept his eye on Sulphur Mountain. Sulphur, unlike most other peaks in the area, was relatively easy to climb and the federal government finally built a trail to its summit.

Jaeggi watched people using that trail and decided that they should have something more waiting for them at the top than the view.

John announced he was going to build a teahouse at the summit and then set out to do just that. The plan was greeted with widespread amusement in the community, and he was kidded that he would sell a lot more tea if he put the teahouse at the bottom of the mountain instead of at the top.

Jaeggi ignored the jibes but, indeed, as he started work on the project it must have seemed occasionally that there was something to the idea of sticking to the bottom.

All the materials and supplies for the project had to be packed on horseback. Even the most basic ingredient for the tea — the water — had to be carried in tanks from a spring halfway up the trail.

By 1940, however, the teahouse was finished. Everything it it was built of logs, including the furnishings. And if John Jaeggi charged five cents a glass for water, visitors were glad to pay it after they learned what effort was needed to get it to them.

For those who made it to the teahouse there was the added bonus, too, of a signed certificate testifying to their feat.

Jaeggi realized, of course, that not everyone had the strength or inclination for the long climb so he built a way-station halfway up the mountain where people could rest — and drink tea — and discuss how they would tackle the full climb to the summit "some other day."

For those who were unable to make even the halfway climb, John outfitted a tractor with a platform and drove them to the way-station.

By 1945 his ideas were proving so successful he doubled the size of the cabin on the summit, creating a panoramic view for his visitors.

When, in 1949, he married Edith Ashton who owned a hotel near one of Sulphur's hot springs, he found a fellow-dreamer and the encouragement to pursue his dream of sharing the mountain with still more people.

Jaeggi made a trip back to Switzerland, then another and another until he had been there 12 times. The trips were no sentimental journeys; they were study trips to investigate the idea of installing a European-type gondola lift on Sulphur Mountain.

He became convinced the idea was practical and that it would make money. But, unhappily, he couldn't find a Canadian investor with the same convictions.

From 1953 to 1957, detailed plans in hand, he made the round of money-men and got turned down cold.

In 1957, frustrated by the indifference of Canadian investors, he turned to Europe and it was finally a group of Swiss businessmen who came up with the money to build the lift.

It was completed in 1958, but Jaeggi himself was to see his dream in action for only three years. In 1961, while on holidays, he was struck by a car and killed.

The gondola, of course, has justified all Jaeggi's dreams. Hundreds of thousands of people have ridden it in the years since it began operation.

It has made it possible for everyone — the aged, the disabled, the very young — to stand on a mountain top. That was what Jaeggi wanted all along.

And the thick cables that hook base to summit serve as a good example for those who would scoff at dreamers.

It took a dreamer, after all, to tie down a mountain.

DANGER AND DISASTER

"He died on the way, in terrible torments — just as had happened to so many of his victims"

—MARIUS BARBEAU,
SPEAKING OF TCHATKA, A STONEY MEDICINE MAN.

* * * *

From time to time, earlier in this book, there have been hints that the Indians of the Canadian Rockies were less than friendly, and much less than helpful, to the white men trying to find their way through the mountains.

The truth is that, for many years of the period during which the west was being settled, the Indians of the mountains hated the white men and would kill anytime they could get away with it. Indeed, at least one trader had to resort to terrible threats to turn smallpox loose among the tribes before his posts could operate in peace.

The reason for the Indians' hatred of the whites sprang from the way the white trader upset the natural balance among the western tribes.

The Stoneys, the Kootenays, the other Indians of the mountains all depended, like the plains Indians, on the buffalo for their main source of food and skins. Tribes like the Stoneys would make at least two expeditions a year down to the plains to hunt the buffalo.

Such expeditions, of course, meant invasions of the traditional territory of the Blackfoot and the Cree — and such violations of frontiers were a challenge to battle.

"Frontiers were not an idle question for the contenders," notes Marius Barbeau, Canada's foremost expert on early Indian life. "They meant safety within their borders where the hunters could scatter at random according to the needs of the chase. In the pursuits of nomadic life, the welfare of all hinged upon the success of the hunt.

"Parties of hunters from various tribes would clash over conflicting claims. No redress could be found but in violence. The security of frontiers once abolished, might have proved the only protection, numbers and cunning, the only pledge of victory."

And it is here, with Barbeau's guidance, that we begin to understand the seeds of the mountain Indians' hatred of the white man. For the coming of the white man tipped the scales of battle. The white man moved in from east to west, bringing the rifle and bullet and gunpowder with him. The Indians of the mountains were the last to get the modern weaponry.

Barbeau paints the painful results:

"In the earlier encounters, the Crees, and then the Blackfoot, had the upper hand. They had secured the coveted firearms from the traders.

"The Blackfoot were the Bedouins of the prairies. Their numbers and boldness gave them the ascendency over other nations, and they never relented in the defence of their vast domains, which extended from the Red River to the Rocky Mountains and from the sources of the Missouri to the Saskatchewan.

"Their war and hunting parties were the terror of the land. In their innumberable encounters with the scattered parties of Cree, Stoney and Kootenay poachers, they were generally victorious. And bitterness sank deep everywhere. The toll of lives grew heavier as time went by. The confused threads of murder and revenge could no longer be unravelled.

"Neither were the territorial claims of the Blackfoot beyond dispute. Were they not themselves intruders from the east long ago?

"The Kootenays and the Flatheads, among others, claimed that the privilege of hunting the buffalo had come down to them from their forefathers. Though they now lived across the mountains, they had always largely depended upon it for subsistence. From childhood they had migrated twice a year in family groups down the mountain passes for the same pursuit.

"The mountain tribes as a last resort might have renounced their pretensions, for they were fighting a losing battle, with only bows and arrows to oppose the guns of the marauders of the plains. Game could be found on their own mountain slopes — deer, mountain sheep and goat, bear, wild-fowl and fish.

"But even the tragedy of their dwindling numbers failed to curb their hereditary bias. The buffalo was at stake, and if anyone hinted at withdrawal from the bad lands, they stubbornly replied that while a single one of their warriors remained alive they should do as their forefathers had done. No right should be relinquished.

"Firearms were the cause of all their misfortunes, since only the Blackfoot could procure them from the North West Company at Fort-des-Prairies, east of the mountains.

"The Kootenays and their allies, the Flatheads, the Coeur-d'Alenes and the Shuswaps, entertained the most violent hatred against the white men for their harmful if unintentional favouritism."

This situation continued until about 1812, when Thompson and other white explorers and traders managed to break trails into the country of the mountain tribes.

These tribes decided to swallow their hatred for the time being — because the white men wanted beaver and were willing to give firearms in return. With these firearms, the mountain tribes believed, vengeance could be taken at last against the Blackfoot.

It was Thompson who recorded the reaction of one Salish chief to the new situation:

"We have now twenty tents of women who have no husbands, with their children, whose fathers are in the Land of Spirits, and as many tents of aged women whose sons have fallen in battle.

"We have all noticed the arrival of the white man among us for these three years bringing us guns, ammunition and shods of iron for the heads of our arrows.

"Before their arrival we were pitiful and could not defend ourselves. But we are now as well armed as our enemies and our last great battle has obliged them to give up to us great parts of our lands for hunting the bison.

"Now we do not fear to war with them."

The Indian of the mountains would not learn to love the white intruder, but he would tolerate him in exchange for the tools of long-awaited revenge.

And revenge there was, bloody revenge that caught the Blackfoot by surprise, produced bloody and brutal battle from which fewer and fewer warriors — on either side — returned to sing by the fires of their own people.

The hatred of the mountain tribes and the brutality of the Blackfoot produced horrors of conflict and torture that almost exceed human imagination.

Ross Cox, a trader, recorded a grim example of the horrors of this war of bloody revenge. It was Christmas Day in 1812 and the Flatheads were torturing a Blackfoot captured in battle. The behavior of the Flatheads and the Blackfoot alike are typical of many similar — and equally horrible — incidents of the time.

"The Flatheads had gathered around the fire to witness the spectacle. Some of them heated an old gun barrel until it had turned red and then burnt stripes as if to make a pattern on the legs, the thighs, the cheeks and the neck of the prisoner, who stood perfectly motionless against a tree to which he was tied.

"Then they cut the flesh about his nails and separated his finger joints one by one. The Blackfoot never winced. Instead he laughed and goaded them on to further efforts.

"'My heart is strong,' he would say; 'you cannot hurt me, you are like fools. Try it again; you don't know how to do it. We torture your relatives far better, because we make them cry aloud like children.'

"A Flathead, who had lost one eye in an encounter years before, was standing sullenly near the fire. So the prisoner taunted him: 'It was by my arrow that you lost your eye. Do you remember?' Thereupon the one-eyed brave darted at him and gouged one of his eyes out of its socket for revenge.

"Undisturbed the Blackfoot now looked with his remaining eye at another of his tormentors and said, 'It was

I who killed your brother and scalped your father. Have you so soon forgotten?' At this provocation the Flathead warrior sprung up like a panther, scalped his insulter and would have plunged his knife into his heart had he not been advised to desist.

"It was now the turn of the head-chief to be insulted by the bleeding prisoner at the stake. 'It was I that made your wife a slave last year. We put out her eyes, tore out her tongue and treated her like a dog.'

"A shriek of rage greeted these words. The chief seized his gun and before the sentence was complete shot a ball through the prisoner's heart, thus ending his frightful torments."

From the need for weapons, the mountain Indians developed a respect — of sorts — for the power of the white man, whose mysterious allies across the seas could supply more and more of what was needed.

"This 'respect,' coupled with the blood-hatred the mountain Indians had for their enemies of the plains, combined — seemed to distill itself — in the veins of one man, a Stoney named Tchatka, whose grim ghost must still haunt the passes of the Canadian Rockies.

* * * *

Tchatka was many things in his life and left many legacies to his own people, the Stoney Indians of the Canadian Rockies. The legacies are mixed.

He left, on the positive side, a return to respect and pride for the Stoney at a time when the Blackfoot were humiliating them on all fronts.

On the negative side, he left a reputation for treachery, cowardice and disgrace that haunts his name to the present day.

As a youth, Tchatka travelled with his people onto the

prairies in their search for the buffalo. On these expeditions, as the 1700's were turning into the 1800's, the Stoney
began to encounter the white man, the traders who were
establishing posts along the fringes of the foothills.

Tchatka fell in awe of the white man, felt the pull of
their ways.

In the months between the expeditions, he would spend
his time day-dreaming of the whites and their powers. On
the expeditions themselves, he spent less and less time on
the hunt and more and more time at the posts, hanging
around the counters where the goods were displayed, feeling in his hands the strange shapes and 'medicine' of the
white man's goods.

Most Indians were curious about the white man and
his ways, but usually such curiosity soon passed off. But
in Tchatka, the curiosity only grew stronger day by day.

This young Stoney and his curiosity were soon noticed
by the traders. They found his interest ingratiating and
his manner both clever and polite.

Tchatka was particularly liked by the French-Canadian
voyageurs, who found his attempts to learn to speak their
language both impressive and amusing. They named him
Le Gaucher, "the left-handed one," and gave him as much
friendship as voyageurs ever gave to Indians.

The young Stoney's preoccupation with the ways of the
whites was noticed by his own people and met with their
strong disapproval.

Tchatka was a son of a large and powerful family, destined by birth and ability both, to be a leader of his people.
This concern for the ways of the still-hated white man
displeased his elders.

By tradition, Tchatka should have gone into the wilds,
braved the hardships alone and emerged a hunter and a
warrior. His uncles pressed him to follow tradition, to

develop through toil and privation the ability and courage to be a leader of his people.

Tchatka refused and was branded both lazy and a coward, though — at this time — he really was neither.

"The truth is," says Marius Barbeau of Tchatka, "that he cared little for pelts and scalping, the ruling ambition of the time. He had notions of his own. His imagination was ablaze with the new ways of life, the ways of the white strangers from the land of sunrise.

"He often resorted to the nearest trading post, forsaking his relatives for prolonged periods. By sheer persistence he managed to learn many truths, many lies, and to unravel many puzzles.

"He finally penetrated the mysteries of the gun casting death at a distance, of powder tearing things to bits when it explodes, and of poison slowly bringing death when it is consumed with foods.

"Above all, he never tired of listening to the tales of another world. The French servants around the stores were fond of telling stories. He sat gaping at what they said of vast wars across the seas, of boundless armies, of guns the size of trees, of generals commanding thunder and lightning, of witchcraft producing wonders, and of kings and princes of fairyland basking in splendor and glory.

"The ambition some day to contemplate all these marvels with his own eyes deeply aroused him. But it also dawned upon his, after many disappointments, that the trail to the home of the mighty was long, almost endless, and strewn with pitfalls.

"He could not very long entertain the hope of becoming a white man himself or, even, living like a white man. Indians, it was easy to see, were not really wanted at the forts, except to procure furs, fish and buffalo meat from their own hunting grounds. And his services as a messenger and guide did not seem sufficiently appreciated. He finally gambled on his last chance one day."

The gamble, as Barbeau records, was disastrous.

"A chief's daughter in his own country always married a chief's son. That was the custom. He himself was of good lineage, the nephew of Walking Bow, whose fame as a powerful warrior had spread from the lakes to the mountains. And the chief-trader's daughter, he knew well, was still unwed. More than once he had seen her, watched her; he had gazed lovingly at her as she smiled to him. That is why he made up his mind.

"She would be his bride and thereafter he would live at the post, with the white men. So he came with presents for the would-be father-in-law. His proposal was listened to according to etiquette. But the bridal presents were returned before the morrow, to his utter dismay. He had thus courted defeat.

"In the face of humiliation he managed to curb his wounded pride; he stayed on at the post for a while. So deep had been his childish hope that it could be smothered only by stages. Then a feeling of revenge crept into his heart, only to be silenced. An Indian is never in a hurry.

"He turned away from the land of promise, slowly, very slowly. His uncles were still waiting for him on the prairies. To them he would return. He started off at night, unseen, disheartened. The heavy bundle on his back contained what was left of his former hopes, rich possessions for his life to come — tobacco, a beaver hat, a red sash, a bright calico shirt, pills of slow and deadly poison, a double-bladed knife in a sheath, gun powder in buffalo horns and a prayer-book full of magic signs."

Despite the disaster and humiliation of his foolish attempt to enter the white man's world by marriage, Tchatka had not lost his ambition for greatness.

All that had changed was that he would seek another road, another kind of greatness. The contents of the pack on his back would play an important part in the new plan he had formed in his mind during the long days at the post after his failure there.

When Tchatka returned to his own people, Barbeau points out, "he was no longer an inexperienced youth.

"The cunning exploitation of his new knowledge and strange crafts helped to enhance his prestige among his nomadic folk.

"Shrewdness was his supreme gift, if ever it was in an Indian. He possessed the white man's 'power' every one could see. Charms and amulets worked miracles in his hands. He muttered incantations at night and communed with the spirits above, the powerful Manitous from the east. The potency of his magic bundle in itself was enough to inspire respect of friend and foe alike.

"Prophecy had always induced timid believers to submit in advance to the dictates of fate. No one dared resist the supernatural powers. To Tchatka it appealed as the easiest means for him to achieve domination. So he became a seer and sorcerer."

Tchatka courted the seers and other medicine men of the Stoney people. He learned what he could of their secrets and supplemented them with the bag of tricks he had brought back with him from the post. He sought out and won to his cause young men who were willing to serve him unquestioningly as disciples — and as spies.

All during this period while he was building a base for his power, he was careful not to risk his life in the too-frequent battles with the Blackfoot. He always stayed on the sidelines, a fast horse ready to carry him away if the tide of battle turned against the Stoney.

To any who dared mutter "cowardice" at this, Tchatka would simply reply that: "I am not a fighter, I never will be. My power is in my medicine."

Soon there were few who questioned the strength of this "medicine" for Tchatka had become a great sorcerer. As Barbeau explains:

"Future events he could foretell as if reading them out of his prayer-book. His uncanny wisdom knew no bounds. He could see far away beyond the skyline. What the others failed to detect were the means at his command, the young spies who served him as secret messengers to get wind of news. Fair probabilities were a safe guide to his foresight; so his predictions seldom failed."

The main obstacle that faced Tchatka now, in his search for power, was that rigid custom dictated who would rule the Stoney. This custom depended hugely on a man's ability as a warrior, the scalps he had taken, the wounds he had suffered and afflicted. Tchatka had taken no scalps and had neither suffered wound nor given it.

Tchatka set out to overcome this obstacle, to win his way onto the ruling council, not by valor but by guile. The tool he chose to use was his aging uncle, Walking Bow.

It took a long campaign of diplomacy and guile, but finally Tchatka won his uncle to his cause. And such was the prestige of Walking Bow that when he proposed that precedent be defied and his nephew admitted to the ruling circle, none questioned and all agreed.

Tchatka, of course, wasn't out simply to sit among the rulers, he wanted to be the ruler of the rulers. And there were many ahead of him, men who had won precedent with time, courage and wisdom. Many excelled him in matters of both war and peace.

Again, however, Tchatka had a plan — this time a cruel

plan. He would combine his 'gift' for foretelling the future and the pills of poison he had in his medicine bag.

Again, Barbeau details the results.

"Thus it came about that in prophetic spells he would say: 'This chief has not long to live; so my Manitou has told me.' And the unfortunate leader whose name had been uttered would fall the victim of a mysterious ailment after weeks, sometimes months, of mental agony. All his rivals disappeared in the same way, one after another.

"Suspicion and the desire of retaliation more than once brought peril near him. Anger smouldered in many breasts. But he inspired fear, as one who can dispose of life. Many were they who thought it best to propitiate him by the offer of presents, buffalo meat, horses and trophies.

"Walking Bow, the head-chief, at times had to shield him against rivals and foes at home. He used his influence to help him in his rapid rise to power. No one dared oppose his will, for his lofty stature, his bravery and violence defied resistance. Scalps taken from the enemy adorned his head-dress, his robe, his spear and the saddle of his steed.

"Tchatka more than any other feared his anger. By flattery and deceit, by subservience to all his desires and fancies, he succeeded in winning his confidence and friendship. They often travelled together and gave one another feasts and banquets in which the greatest harmony always prevailed.

"Jealous as Tchatka was of Walking Bow's rank, he could not dispense with him until all those opposing his march to the supreme power in the tribe had been removed..."

For Tchatka, grown now powerful and cruel, was out to supplant his benefactor as head chief.

Walking Bow did not know his peril and Tchatka was careful to give no sign. His long practice at the trading post, in hiding his true feelings and disappointment, was being put to deadly use.

Finally, the day came when Tchatka saw his chance to make a deadly move.

"His emissiaries," writes Barbeau, "sighted a camp of Blackfoot hunters one day. From their description he knew that the warriors of his own tribe could surprise them and win a decisive victory. The moment had come for him to fortell the event and to strike a supreme blow.

"He invited his uncle to a feast and presented him with a poisoned dish of buffalo tongues. The fatal meal having been consumed to the last mouthful according to the custom, it could not fail to produce its effect after a few hours. Thus would be removed the last obstacle left in his path."

Tchatka, having made the key move, now had to act quickly and daringly to gain control — for in poisoning Walking Bow he was not only removing his last obstacle to power, he was also removing his main defence against his enemies.

Barbeau documents Tchatka's cunning — and extraordinary luck — in vivid terms:

"Walking Bow had no sooner departed after the banquet than his nephew summoned all the leading warriors to his lodge in great haste. Word went round that grave events impended, for the Manitous had given warning.

Tchatka appeared before them attired for the first time with all his finery — the flowing calico shirt, the red sash around his waist, the tall beaver hat on his head and the open prayer book in his hand.

"His Manitou, the Thunder, stood in the centre of the lodge near the fire, under the shape of a magic stone painted red and surrounded by a fence of short sticks.

"At the sight of these strange objects, the assembly sat dumb with awe, and the inspired seer delivered his prophecy as if under a spell.

"He could see far away and tell what was to happen. A camp of the enemy stood near a river, a few days' journey. The Stoneys could take it by surprise and capture many scalps. Time had come for them at last to avenge previous defeats.

"But that was not all. A most valiant brave present at the assembly would fall this very night never to rise again, and at the very moment of his death the Thunder Manitou would blow up to pieces with a dreadful noise to accompany the departing soul into the world of spirits. Another chief, more favoured by the Manitous, would step into his place for the good of all the nation.

"A dismal silence greeted these prophetic words. Victory and revenge naturally aroused their expectations, but in spite of it all dread appeared on every countenance.

"Who was to fall that very night? No one could tell, as many leaders were almost the equals of the head-chief. Not even Walking Bow had any clear idea of his own doom.

"But no doubt could be entertained as to the prophecy; too many others had already proved true. The warriors withdrew in silence and gloom. Dark apprehension invaded the camp with the shades of night.

"At midnight a messenger came running to Tchatka's lodge. 'Come, come! Walking Bow is ill, very ill.'

"But the wily seer could not so easily be induced to affront danger. His uncle, he knew, now suspected his treachery. He would stretch him dead at his feet while he still possessed enough strength.

"So he replied, 'Go and tell him my visit would not help him. And I could not at this moment leave my Manitou alone.'

"The prey of terrible convulsions, Walking Bow declared

to the friends and relatives surrounding him, 'I suspect him, my nephew.'

"Consternation and tumult spread to every lodge. Some warriors uttered frightful yells, vowed speedy revenge and resorted to Tchatka's quarters.

"The seer, still attired in his finery, stood alone near the fire, facing his Thunder Manitou. At the news of his uncle's ordeal he pretended real sorrow, and trembling at the sight of uplifted tomahawks he enjoined the avengers to stay their arm and listen once more to his words.

"'Relatives and friends,' he said, 'Walking Bow is my uncle and my friend; we are of the same blood and eat from the same dish. How could I injure him who has always given me his help and confidence?

"'He was the strongest of warriors at sunset and now is grappling with death. This shows how powerful are the Manitous. What could I do? If I predicted his death it is because the very spirit of Thunder was speaking through my mouth.'

"As the tomahawks were still threatening him, he pleaded again, 'You disbelieve my words? If you do, look at my Manitou, the red stone; look at it closely, for what I have predicted will happen. It will blow up in bits with a terrible noise when the great warrior dies. And when it has happened, will you again lift your arms against me? Will you distrust me as you do now?'

"The sullen warriors drew inside the lodge hesitatingly, one by one. Like mute sentinels they sat around the mysterious red stone. As they waited in dread for its disappearance the fire grew dim and the feeble light shivered on their sinister faces. Ghost-like shadows danced on the sloping sides of the lodge.

"Runners from Walking Bow's tent came by at intervals, shouting, 'The chief utters naught but shrieks of rage against his nephew ... He is in convulsions ... He is growing more feeble ... His speech is gone ... He is in agony...'

"Cries of despair responded to the last message: 'He is dead!'

"And the red stone by the fire burst into a thousand fragments with the noise of thunder. It filled the lodge with fire and cinders, severely wounding those who sat near and frightening the others into a wild stampede.

"Tchatka's powers once more stood vindicated in the eyes of all. The feeling of revenge gave way to one of terror and reverence. No one approached him but with respect. His Manitou, being the Thunder, he now received the name of 'Great Medicine'."

What Tchatka had done involved no magic at all — just a good sense of stage management and a healthy dose of the gunpowder he had carried from the trading post inside a horn.

Days before, in total secrecy, Tchatka had drilled a hole in the stone and packed it with close to a pound of black powder. When the Manitou was set up in his lodge, he had left an inconspicuous trail of powder leading to the stone, and when the news of his uncle's death came he was waiting in the shadows with a glowing ember to touch off the fuse.

He had accomplished the first part of his prediction. Now it was up to him to bring off the second — the victory over the Blackfoot hunters — and his grasp on the control of the Stoneys would be complete.

There were still many, particularly among the close relatives and friends of Walking Bow, who would have moved against Tchatka if they had dared. And, as Tchatka knew, they would move if he couldn't make his prediction of victory over the Blackfoot come true.

Tchatka again began an elaborate production. He went

into seclusion in his lodge the day after Walking Bow's death. No one but his 'disciples' dared approach him and no one else in the tribe suspected that these disciples were bringing him updated reports on the Blackfoots' movements.

The second day saw the isolation continue and so did the third day. Tchatka's enemies began to see this inaction as a sign of failure and slowly started agitating for revenge against Tchatka.

Before they could muster enough power to move, however, word was circled through the camp to 'Watch the Great-Medicine Lodge!'

Tchatka was getting ready to go into action on the decisive phase of his plan and, on sunset of the third day, nature intervened to give his stage management a hand.

A storm began building from the northeast. Dark clouds moved in, lightning flashed and thunder rumbled.

The Stoneys stirred uneasily, remembering that Tchatka's Manitou was the Thunder.

Tchatka, like the others, was watching the approach of the storm and playing its timing for full dramatic effect.

As the time came to move, Barbeau notes, Tchatka showed all the sense of a veteran Broadway director.

"When the storm was about to break out, at midnight, a deep sound from the seer's lodge startled the people, a sound like that of a large water drum. It was loud enough to be heard throughout the camp. Tchatka's voice rose gradually and the meaningless syllables he uttered were those of a new incantation.

"Runners now summoned the warriors to the Great-Medicine lodge, and while the assembly gathered according to etiquette, wind, rain and thunder roared mightily in unison.

"At the back of the lodge stood Tchatka, a headress

of swan's down on his head. His left hand deftly beat a tchantcheega— a huge drum made of a hollow tree, about three feet high, with a goat skin tightly stretched and pegged at one end. Powerful new Manitous, Grizzly-Bear and Buffalo-Bull were painted yellow and red on the bleached skin, and on the wood all around a large number of small human faces were traced in black outline to represent Blackfoot heads.

"Apparently unaware of the warriors' entry into the lodge he continued his incantation for a while, and then, when all were seated in a half-circle opposite him, he kneeled down in the manner of a Christian and offered thanksgivings to the Great Spirit and his new protectors, the Grizzly and the Buffalo, for their many favors.

"Standing up defiantly while thunder and storm raged outside, he intoned a vehement war song. His lips were dyed red with vermillion to indicate that the spirit of war was in his breath and that his thirst was only for blood, the blood of the enemy..."

Satisfied that his audience was properly primed, Tchatka began a speech designed to stir their hottest emotions. For the past three days, he claimed, he had left this world and gone to the world of the spirits and ghosts.

"There, I have beheld frightful scenes, I have heard sighs, moans and lamentations. I have walked among the dead..."

Among the dead, he told the warriors, were those of the Stoney warriors, women and children who had been slain by the Blackfoot. To the trembling warriors, he told the tale of the dead:

"Let those who have ears listen once for all. There is no time to lose. The souls of our massacred relatives cannot go to the land of rest until they are avenged in blood. They wander up and down in the dark through barren deserts, without food for subsistence. They are cold, thirsty and hungry.

"We are the cause of their torments, since we dare not start on the war path against our foes, and they complain of our forgetfulness.

"A friendly soul touched my hand and said, 'Tchatka, we know you. You are a great sorcerer. It is in your power to bring our deliverance. When you return to our people tell them what you have seen. In your teepee you will find your new Manitou, the drum Tchantcheega. Arise and beat it when the storm breaks out, at night. We shall be near. Tell the warriors to be ready, to start on the war-path at daybreak, for thirty Blackfeet tents stand at the source of the Milk River, not far away. Victory shall be yours. Revenge will end our sufferings.'

"Thus the ghosts have spoken, and when I recovered

my senses I found the drum Tchantcheega at my feet. Now you have heard the truth, friends and relatives. What shall you do?"

It was a question that need hardly have been asked. Tchatka had cunningly touched the vein of deep hatred and longing for revenge that the Stoney had inside them. To a man, the warriors leapt to their feet and screamed the war cry and soon were circling the fire in the scalp dance.

By daybreak, 400 Stoney warriors, war-painted and their arrows sharpened, were ready to set out. They waited by their saddled horses for Tchatka to appear and lead them into battle, but he did not come.

A delegate was sent to his lodge to ask him to take the lead as the vision had foreseen. But he refused, reminding the delegate that only yesterday they were ready to slay him, and besides he was a seer, not a warrior. Choose someone else, he suggested.

Delegate followed delegate to plead with him and Tchatka toyed with each. It was only when the rest of the elders of the tribe had pledged him unquestioning confidence and accepted him as head-chief of the whole tribe that he agreed to go — which had been his plan all along.

The war party was on the trail for some days, Tchatka at the lead with his drum Tchantcheega fastened behind the saddle.

On the trail, he bragged that "If my predictions come true we shall tear from the enemy as many scalps as there are on my drum. We shall see the great chief of the Blackfoot as he appears here, without scalp and without hands."

Tchatka's scouts finally located the Blackfoot encampment and the whole force of Stoneys encircled it by night.

At daybreak, the bloodbath began — but all the Blackfoot warriors were away. There were only women and children and old men to slay, but to the worked-up Stoneys a scalp was a scalp.

The war party, hands bloody and scalps dangling from their saddles, was soon on the trail again. They had killed many, but where were the Blackfoot warriors — particularly the "great chief" Tchatka had predicted would be slain?

As it turned out, it was the Blackfoot who found the Stoneys, not the other way around. There was a shower overnight and, as the party took up the trail again, the way was obscured in fog.

Out of the fog, suddenly, came the Blackfoot and, as Barbeau records it, "Before Tchatka had time to think of his own safety, he found himself enveloped in the midst of fighters, unable to seek shelter anywhere.

"His horse tumbled under him and he fell to the ground. A Blackfoot of lofty stature and great strength hurled his spear at him. The weapon grazed his head and sank quivering into the earth. Then he dashed for him, knife in hand.

"Tchatka by then had had time to jump to his feet and draw his double-bladed knife from its sheath.

"Coward as he was he found himself compelled against his own choice to fight for his life. And he did fight with great boldness and skill. He seized the wrist of his adversary and managed to hold the knife off his own body.

"When the battle in the front line had ceased, the Stoneys returned to look for their chief, whom they had lost sight of. They found him struggling arm in arm, on the ground, with a powerful enemy. The Blackfoot at this moment disengaged his arm and lifted his knife for a fatal thrust.

"But a tomahawk from behind stretched him unconscious, and Tchatka in his turn raised his own knife, shouting, 'Friends, behold the chief of the Blackfoot!'" and he plunged the blade into his heart. With the same blood-stained knife he scalped him and cut his hands off, to fulfil the prophecy which has ever been retold among the Stoneys.

"Then he said, 'Here was Bear's Foot, the terror of our own people for so many years,' and he pulled off the white man's medal which hung from his neck as a mark of distinction. His warriors, in commemoration of this, now conferred upon him the name of Minayonka, 'the Knife-holder'.

"After so swift and overwhelming a victory they all returned home loaded with trophies. The exultation of the whole tribe ran so high that public rejoicing lasted for a whole moon; scalp dances, songs and thanksgivings were repeated a hundred times.

"Tchatka's new name Minayonka, 'the Knife-holder', was celebrated in every mouth. Never had the nation known such a famous leader, warrior and sorcerer all at once. His ambition was fulfilled at last, for he was entrusted with the supreme, undivided authority over the affairs of the nation."

Tchatka, true to his character, was not content to let mere glory and power suffice. As Barbeau remarks:

"To mark his triumph in his own way, Tchatka selected three wives on the same day, without even considering that two of them were already betrothed to two of his influential warriors. Protests were not heeded, and the parents of the brides felt so honoured by the head chief's choice that they forgot their former pledges and took their daughters to his lodge as soon as an invitation was received.

"To curb discontent and restore peace in every household Tchatka decided to start for the hunt, but not without leaving orders to the most trusted of his partisans to poison his two rival pretenders in his absence.

"Upon his return he feigned surprise at the news of the mysterious death of the pretenders, and only concluded, 'So it always happens. The Manitous have done it. Let those who contradict me, who despise my power, remember it. Their danger is near.'"

For 40 years, Tchatka held the Stoney people under his complete domination — both by fear and by his skill at warfare. From the stories he had heard at the trading-post so many years before, he had developed a keen understanding of warfare: the need for intelligence-gathering and the way in which forces can be used in mass attacks.

Memories of his humiliation at the trading post, now called Fort Union, haunted him constantly, but he kept swallowing the taste of revenge out of fear of the white man's power.

But the day finally came when this fear gave way to a pressing need and he set forth on the path to his final undoing.

What set him on the path was an unexpected defeat at the hands of the Blackfoot. For once, Tchatka's spies had failed and the Stoney were taken by surprise on a war raid in 1830. More than 60 of his warriors were slain and another 60 were taken prisoner, to be returned to torture and death at the hands of the Blackfoot.

It didn't help that Tchatka himself had fled the scene of the battle when the tide turned against the Stoney and his excuse that his new Manitou, the Badger, had carried him away, fell feebly on the ears of the many Stoney who were mourning the death of husbands and sons.

Tchatka decided that he had to act — and quickly — to "cover the dead" with a victory of some kind, so that the defeat would be forgotten. As usual, his love of the theatrical played a strong part in his new strategy. Again it is Barbeau who offers the best description of the incident

— and of the human compassion that brought Tchatka to disaster instead of treacherous victory.

"He retired to his sacred lodge in anticipation of new dreams, new visions of victory. This time his inner determination moved against the white traders at Fort Union, the post where his early ambitions had encountered defeat. Badger, his Manitou, had ceased to serve his purpose, so he called back his old-time protectors, Thunder, Grizzly-Bear and Buffalo-Bull. The mere allusion to their familiar names would spur confidence and instil new vigour in faltering hearts.

"Summoned to his lodge in the name of powerful Manitous, the tribal leaders and the warriors heard of a new war adventure, to the east. Untold riches were to fall into their hands without bloodshed, in a single night. Spoils would be so abundant that the horses of the whole tribe could not drag them all on their travois. The new prophecy was bound to be true, for Tchatka's reliable Manitous of old now had returned from their prolonged retreat.

"The raid contemplated against the trading establishment, Fort Union, was entirely devoid of risk. The occupants had no reason to be suspicious of standing on their guard, since the friendliest relations with all natives had always prevailed.

"The prize lay within the grasp of the Stoneys, but on one condition only: they must unreservedly agree with the plan of their chief and remain blindly faithful to the very end. They all pledged themselves to the most servile obedience. Brighter days were in sight.

"Escorted by three hundred of his best warriors, Tchatka started in the direction of the fort, which stood on the prairie not many days off. His scheme was to approach the traders with the customary amenities, then overwhelm their small force at night and take possession of the two years' stock of goods which had just arrived for the needs of the fur trade.

"The Stoneys were greeted at the fort as on former occasions. The calumet was lit and handed over by the chief trader to the leading visitor, Tchatka, who passed it on to his followers without drawing a whiff of the white smoke like the others.

"This apparent oversight was barely noticeable, and the usual precaution of disarming the native visitors for the night and placing their weapons under lock and key was not even resorted to; Tchatka's old-time friendship for the white people sufficed to remove all suspicion...

"By a shrewdly concerted plan, the dusky warriors had arranged to retire to the various rooms of the establishment for the night. To Tchatka and a faithful follower was reserved the keeping of a small detached dwelling within the fort's enclosure. In that house resided a white woman whose life he wanted to spare, for he remembered her from the time of his youth. She was to be his prisoner, perhaps his wife in spite of the fact that she was married — for he had never forgotten her as the late chief-factor's daughter, the very one who had been ignominiously refused him at the time of his juvenile illusions, long ago. All the other residents were to be massacred at a given signal before the break of day.

"A Stoney runner whose sister was married to a white servant at the fort could not silence his brotherly feelings. He invited her in deep secrecy to resort to his room for the night. But, as she could not understand his meaning, he explained that all her white friends were to perish before sunrise. She promised to follow him, but instead hastened to confide in her husband, whom she wanted to save from death.

"The plot at this stage could no longer remain a secret.

It reached the authorities in the twinkle of an eye.

"Orders from headquarters were whispered around quietly and swiftly. Every white man was armed to the teeth, the guns were loaded, and the two bastions were made ready for siege. All hopes for a successful resistance might have been vain but for a singularly fortunate coincidence; a number of Canadian employees (voyageurs), altogether about eighty, had arrived a few days before from the northern posts to receive their share of the newly arrived trading goods. Their presence now made a great difference; it offered the only safeguard of the moment.

"Mr. Denig, the chief trader, summoned Tchatka and a few of his accomplices to appear before him, as soon as all preparations were complete. He reproached them with their treachery. They wanted to stab their own friends and protectors in the back. How could he place further reliance in them, since they acted as liars and traitors? They deserved only contempt.

Their choice now was either to quit the fort forthwith or be destroyed by the big guns that were levelled at them from every side. Dumbfounded, the warriors instantly decided to withdraw, even without consulting their guilty leader, who was deeply vexed and confused at the failure of his wonderful plot.

"The blow to the great seer's prestige among his own people was decisive, final. Anger and defiance could no longer be suppressed, particularly since the supply of poison in his medicine bag was nearly exhausted."

Tchatka was to make one final bid to restore his prestige, an ill-conceived raid on the Mandans which resulted in the loss of all the Stoney war party except Tchatka himself, who managed to flee the carnage on foot.

It was his last attempt to reverse the downhill curve his cruel career had taken. He was now an old man and, if the Stoney still held his past deeds in esteem, the man who did them was no longer a power among his people.

In the autumn of 1843, the old man made a choice. He could not go on living without power and there was no way left to grasp power. He reached into his old medicine bag for the little poison he had left.

Even in this final act, however, Tchatka could not resist the appeal of the theatrical. It was the time of the fall gathering, the time when all the tribes brought in their furs to the trading posts. As the Stoney prepared to leave their village, Tchatka reported a vision:

"My end is fast approaching. Before many sunsets my soul shall depart for the unseen prairies of our dead relatives."

The Stoney came once again to the gates of Fort Union and the old seer shook Denig by the hand.

"Friend," said Tchatka, "here is the place where I have always wanted to live, to die, among the friends of my youth. Never again shall I visit your wonderful fort. Never shall I see the country of the white man across the sea. My time is passed."

Denig was curious and uncomfortable at these statements. The old chief seemed in good health and inquiries among the Stoney confirmed the impression that Tchatka had not been ill.

That night, when the Stoney gathered to feast, Tchatka prepared his own dish and ate it to the last drop. Then, while the others were dancing by the fire, he retired alone to his lodge.

By morning he was spitting blood. By afternoon he was in terrible convulsions. By night he was dead.

It was a cruel but fitting end for a man who had tried to seize the power of both the white and Indian world in so ruthless a way.

There were many before Tchatka who had been evil, and there would be many men after — thieves and murderers who would also be evil. But in the mountains of our west, no man so distilled the essence of the worst of the encounter of the two cultures.

It is an ironic footnote that Tchatka's own people decided, in the end, to forget his murdering and treachery and remember instead that he had led them to many victories and much revenge.

To this day, the place where he is buried is venerated by his people and his name is venerated as "the greatest man that ever visited our nation."

* * * *